60

second
solutions

ORGANIZATION

60 second solutions
ORGANIZATION

JEFF DAVIDSON

David and Charles

A DAVID & CHARLES BOOK
© F&W Media International, LTD 2011

David & Charles is an imprint of F&W Media
International, LTD
Brunel House, Forde Close, Newton Abbot, TQ12 4PU, UK

F&W Media International, LTD is a subsidiary of
F+W Media, Inc.
4700 East Galbraith Road, Cincinnati, OH 45236

First published in the UK in 2011

Text copyright © Jeff Davidson 2011

The material in this book has been previously published
in *The 60 Second Organizer 2nd Edition*, published by
Adams Media, 2008.

Jeff Davidson has asserted the right to be identified as
author of this work in accordance with the Copyright,
Designs and Patents Act, 1988.

A catalogue record for this book is available from the
British Library.

ISBN-13: 978-1-4463-0045-9 paperback
ISBN-10: 1-4463-0045-5 paperback

Printed in Finland by Bookwell for
F&W Media International LTD,
Brunel House, Forde Close, Newton Abbot, TQ12 4PU, UK

10 9 8 7 6 5 4 3 2 1

Senior Acquisitions Editor: Freya Dangerfield
Assistant Editor: Felicity Barr
Project Editor: Cheryl Brown
Proofreader: Freya Dangerfield
Design Manager: Sarah Clark
Production Controller: Bev Richardson

F+W Media publish high quality books on a wide range
of subjects.
For more great book ideas visit: www.rubooks.co.uk

CONTENTS

INTRODUCTION

Do you feel overwhelmed by the never-ending lists of responsibilities and tasks that need to be completed? Are you caught up in an unyielding cycle of work that makes you feel as if you are always running behind? Do you find yourself brushing up against deadlines, often completing projects after they are due? If so, you are not alone.

60 Second Solutions Organization has been written with you in mind. These simple tips can help you to restore order to any area of your life, whether it is your desk or office, your wardrobe or your home, your car or your garage. The idea is that you should dip in to find a solution that works for the situation you find yourself in. From workplace to cyberspace, from our personal life to our professional one, we could all benefit from being more organized. All you need to understand are a few guiding principles and hands-on techniques as outlined in this indispensable little volume.

continuing to live a disorganized life makes as much sense as studying 10 hours for a 15-minute quiz

DISORGANIZATION IS COSTLY

The negative effects of disorganization may be wreaking havoc on your career, though you may not even realize it. Being disorganized sends out a negative message to others. Your colleagues may be reluctant to ask you for help because your office looks so out of control. This may apply to you if recognize any of the following behaviours.

- Do you end up leaving important tasks unfinished because you are not sufficiently organized to complete them?
- Are you behind schedule more than others in your company?
- Do you have difficulty finding important documents or files?
- Do you forget about important meetings and appointments?
- Do you have an inability to let go of projects you are working on?
- Does a backlog of outdated material hamper your ability to take advantage of current challenges?
- Does the clutter around you diminish your productivity?
- Are you putting in overtime more frequently than you'd like to?

The above are problems disorganized people know all too well. And if being disorganized is having a negative affect on your career, consider what it might be doing to your personal life. If you suspect that your health and happiness is at stake, it's time to face up to the task of getting organized.

disorganization is often associated with stress, anxiety and illness

RESPONDING TO LIFE

Becoming and staying organized requires effort and thought, but in the long term it will save you time and give you peace of mind. However the truth is you have to spend time to save time. It can help to think of getting organized as preparing 'to respond to life'.

No one is born with organizational skills. We all have to learn techniques along the way. The key to becoming and remaining organized is to recognize how valuable it can be to have everything in order. Then you can make the necessary changes to cut through the chaos. I estimate that for most people this will take the equivalent of about three full weekends and four to five weeknights.

being organized is essential to a successful career and a happy home life

Most people have too much stuff and too little space to store it in. But here's an important principle: more space is seldom the answer. Deleting the nonessential from our lives (throwing things away) and filing sensibly what we judge necessary to retain is the only solution. It is almost a guarantee that you are holding on to too many items, stuff you have over collected and things you have over filed. You need to go back through the places and spaces in your life to review what is essential to you.

HOW ORGANIZED ARE YOU?

If you answer 'yes' to any of the following questions, you definitely need to take action now.

Q1 Do you spend 5 minutes or more looking for an email or document?

Q2 Are papers over one month old stacked on your desk?

Q3 Do you have trouble finding an item in your desk that you use frequently?

Q4 Do you feel that you could be organized if you only had more space?

Q5 Do you have piles of magazines and journals you haven't read?

Q6 Do you often find something at the bottom of a pile that you didn't know was there?

Q7 Do you have hundreds of emails accumulating in your inbox?

organizing is an exercise in control, efficiency and peace of mind

Even if you have an ultra-demanding job and considerable professional and personal responsibilities, you can regain control. If you've resolved to get organized, then you're well on the road to achieving your aim.

The author would like to thank subject matter experts for their inspirations: Michael Gershon MD, Barbara Hemphill, Robert Fritz, Nancilee Wydra, Jim Cathcart, Nicholas Lemann, Robert Cooper PhD, Stephen Hawking PhD, Don Aslett, Dr Wayne Dyer, Robert Levasseur, Jaclyn Kostner PhD, and the late David McClelland PhD, Vilfredo Pareto and Earl Nightingale.

part
one

part
one

EMBRACING POWERFUL PERSPECTIVES

SOLUTION 1
ORGANIZATION CAN BE FUN

By choosing to pick up this book, you have clearly shown that you want to improve your life and your career by becoming organized. You have the power to achieve your goal of becoming organized, and to follow through with this in all aspects of your life.

You have the ability to summon your own personal motivation to overcome the challenges and roadblocks in your path. And the good news is that getting things in order can be fun, or satisfying at the very least.

AMAZE YOURSELF

When you actually commit to get organized, you sometimes astonish yourself by how much you can accomplish in a relatively short amount of time. What if you were to spend one day, one morning, or merely the next hour putting things in order? What if you treated the activity as if it had vital importance in your career or personal life? If you considered getting organized to be of great importance then, like other important things in your life, you would do it.

LITTLE AND OFTEN

Make a start today. Examine your desktop, desk drawers, shelves, filing cabinet and storage cupboard to see what you can get rid of. This includes:

- Outdated directories or instruction manuals you won't use again
- Outdated flyers, annual reports, PR materials, announcements, catalogues and invitations
- Magazines more than two years out of date
- Get rid of scraps of paper and rough drafts
- Memos, correspondence, reports and any documents that do not have to be retained

If you don't find anything – search again!

when it comes to getting organized, how you decide to approach the task is up to you

QUICK FIX: MAKE IT FUN

- If you have to rearrange shelves, make a game out of rearranging them efficiently
- If you have to remove piles that have accumulated around the corners of your office, take it on as a challenge
- There is no single 'right way' to do things, so find the way that is enjoyable for you

SOLUTION 2
LEARN YOUR ORGANIZATIONAL ABCs

When you recall any major achievement in your life, such as being accepted to university or completing a tough project at work, you will discover that these accomplishments follow the pattern of antecedent, behaviour and consequence, or the ABC of behavioural change.

Antecedents precede Behaviours and behaviours precede Consequences

To become an organized individual you need to learn your ABCs. When you better understand your motivation for getting organized (antecedent), you can then take the appropriate action (behaviour) that will result in the desired achievement (consequence). It's as easy as ... well ... A, B, C.

Driving along a country road on a warm spring day, you see a stop sign. The sign is the antecedent. The behaviour derived from this is, you stop the car. As a consequence, you obey the law, avoiding the possibility of either an accident. Imagine this same situation, but with a different behaviour. You see a stop sign, and rather than stopping, your behaviour is to ignore it and drive through it. What are the consequences? If no one is around, you might save a couple of seconds and continue on your way. But what if a car is coming the other way ...?

RECOGNIZE YOUR ORGANIZATIONAL ANTECEDENTS

Every goal you've ever set, and every goal that you will set, is based upon an antecedent. The two fundamental antecedents for engaging in behaviours that lead to goal achievement are the recognition of opportunity and the fear of pain.

Opportunity-related reasons:

- To demonstrate competency
- To be recognized as an expert
- To improve your chances for advancement
- To get a pay increase
- To act as a team player
- To use less space at your desk, cubicle or office
- To set an example in your department

Avoidance-of-pain-related reasons:

- To avoid looking like you're swamped
- To comply with your boss's orders and so avoid a reprimand
- To limit time spent searching for misplaced things
- To avoid appearing disorderly to visitors
- To avoid feeling inadequate

BE AN INSPIRATION

Whether your motivation to be organized stems from your wish to live up to others expectations of you, or your desire to have people regard you as being in control, or simply to show someone out there who is convinced you can't do it that you can, when the consequences of your behaviour are positive, your experience can be an antecedent for other people. By setting a good example, you can set your colleagues off on their own ABC journey.

SOLUTION 3
BANK YOUR GOLDEN INSIGHTS

'Ideas are like slippery fish. Unless you write them down, they are going to slip away.'
Earl Nightingale

Do you take the time to organize your thoughts? Do you remember your most original and creative ideas? How many of your light bulb moments have been lost to the back of an envelope, jotted down on a napkin, or scribbled on the back of your hand, but never followed through. These ideas could be your most valuable assets in determining where to devote your time and energy to achieve your goals, so unless you have a way of recording them, you are short-changing yourself.

MAKE TIME FOR GREAT IDEAS
You need to allow yourself the space to determine what you want to achieve. To what type of project are you willing to commit? What areas merit your time and energy? How will you go about accomplishing your goals? Make time to organize the thoughts in your busy mind. To harness your brainpower, any one of the following may be necessary:

- Hold your calls
- Turn off your email
- Post a 'Do not disturb' sign on your door
- Go for a walk
- Take a break
- Make the most of your commute to work time

singularities:
once-only events as
defined by Professor
Stephen Hawking,
celebrated
astrophysicist

*you will not have the same moment of
inspiration twice, so make the most of it*

QUICK FIX: RECORDING THOUGHTS

Park the innovative thoughts you have throughout your day ready to
organize them for action later. Here are a few simple ideas:

- Set up a 'good ideas' file in a notebook, electronic organizer, on
  your hard drive, or even on your mobile phone
- Record ideas on a whiteboard by your desk
- Use a traditional calendar planner to jot down important
  notes or dates
- Send reminder emails to yourself or even to close friends
  and colleagues
- Scan or copy related articles from magazines and documents,
  and make a thought collage
- Use a digital recorder to dictate reminders and transcribe the
  recordings to your note files

SOLUTION 4
CHOOSE TO BE ORGANIZED

How you elect to feel about any situation is always your choice. The act of choosing is a simple but powerful technique that will aid you in becoming and remaining organized.

By making important choices, you automatically redirect yourself to accept that there is nothing you must do; everything is based on your choice. If you choose to keep working on some task, this personal decision is made in the present moment and not based on a prior agenda. The new sense of control over your own life will yield a tremendous sense of inner harmony. So, choose to choose.

Imagine you and your family are sitting in a 10 mile traffic tailback on August Bank Holiday weekend. It's a sweltering day and to top it all the car's air conditioner conks out. You may feel tempted to curse not only the air conditioner but also the car maker, the car in front of you and the car in front of that; in fact whose idea was it to have a family day out after all? But before you blame the baby, remember you could choose to enjoy the time this allows you to spend with your family – roll down the windows, sing a few favourite songs and play a few travel games. In no time at all, you will be on your way again.

QUICK FIX: MAKING A CHOICE

Here are some of the powerful thinking techniques you can keep in mind as you decide to increase your capacity for becoming and remaining organized. To reinforce the choices you make, write them down or type them, or record them and play them back to yourself.

- I choose to easily become and remain organized
- I choose to regard getting organized as an extremely fun and worthwhile activity
- I choose to easily take control of my spaces
- I choose to maintain clarity when facing organizing challenges
- I choose to constantly recognize the areas of life where I'm the master of staying organized
- I choose to easily learn new methods of becoming organized
- I choose to associate with people who are highly organized and will serve as role models, mentors and teachers
- I choose to approach disorganized situations with calmness and clarity
- I choose to readily reward myself for my organizational victories
- I choose to feel good about the efforts I make to get organized
- I choose to embrace challenging situations methodically and effectively
- I choose to be an overall master of personal organization

SOLUTION 5
ASK 'WHO CREATED THAT?'

More times than you probably care to admit, most of the situations relating to disorder in your life were created by you. Take your office, for example. Can you name a space, a surface, or even a single drawer for which you are not responsible?

When you honestly confront this issue, you're bound to concede that you created the mayhem and that you can take control of it too.

STOP BLAMING OTHERS

Perhaps there has been an occasion at work when a colleague changed or rearranged things that once had an order. At home, too, family members may have had some part to play in the

disorganized people believe that things get out of order or get lost or misplaced of their own accord

disorganization you face. However, you are a person of influence and you can control the level of impact that others have on your places and spaces. Your tolerance of disorganized people, either at home or at work, contributes to the general disorder of your environment. This observation is not meant to convince you to seek a new job or a new family, but merely to emphasize that you are the person in control and can effect change.

In his book *The Path of Least Resistance*, author Robert Fritz suggests that you ask yourself a critical question when you're faced with a challenging situation. The question is: Who created that?

SOLUTION 6
LIVE AND LET LEARN

So, you want to be more organized? You may not have a good track record for being organized in the past, but you can make the decision to change all that. Rather than living life looking through a rear-view mirror, you can decide to live in the present, to set yourself organizational goals that might once have seemed way beyond your ability. You can reach those goals once you recognize that the power to achieve them was in you all along.

make clear and confident choices about what you want in the future

Stop thinking, 'I've never been good at organizing,' accept that you may have changed over the years; acknowledge the organizational challenges you have overcome, and look forward to those you have yet to achieve.

In a study published in the 1996 *Annual Review of Psychology*, researchers at Tel Aviv University and the University of Waterloo in Ontario found that: 'people less able to relate the person of the past to the person they are now may be at greater psychological risk, because they are thinking only in the present and their view of the future may not be developed.' In other words, if you're not able to recognize how you've changed since the past, you're likely to let past behaviours unduly influence what you do next.

SOLUTION 7
WORK SMARTER MORE OF THE TIME

It makes sense even in our busiest moments to take a little time to reflect on what we want to accomplish, and to organize our thoughts and actions to achieve those goals. Unless we have an organized structure in place we are in danger of working long, hard hours with little to show for it.

A profound way to 'work smarter' is to learn to follow your inner wisdom and to rely on your instincts more routinely. Decisions based on intuition encompass all of your life experiences and acquired knowledge. If you're figuring out how to organize something, it's often okay to simply start and let your intuition guide you. That's preferable, after all, to not starting at all.

Scientists in the field of neurocardiology have discovered a 'brain in the heart' comprised of more than 40,000 neurons, along with a complex network of neurotransmitters, proteins and support cells. 'This heart brain,' says Robert Cooper, PhD, 'is as large as many key areas of the thinking brain and sufficiently sophisticated to rate as a brain in its own right.' Each heartbeat is linked to the thinking brain and affects both branches of the autonomic nervous system, continually influencing our perceptions and awareness. Cooper continues, 'The heart is not only open to new possibilities, it actively scans for them, ever seeking new, intuitive understanding.'

FOLLOW YOUR GUT INSTINCTS

Pioneering research by physiologists and gastro-enterologists indicates that there is a 'brain' in the intestines. Known as the 'enteric nervous system', it is independent of and interconnected with the brain. It appears that gut instincts are real and warrant listening to.

gut instinct: intuitively knowing when something is right or wrong

for most of the organizing challenges you face, you probably have a strong idea how best to proceed

QUICK FIX: COMPUTER SMART

If you want to master your computer systems rather than be a slave to them, you need to take a more organized and methodical approach.

- Schedule time to get to know a new software program and dispense with the trial-and-error approach you usually rely on
- Ask the office 'expert' – or at least someone who knows more than you do – to run through the key features and make notes
- Keep your summary card of instructions for the key functions you require pasted on your desktop
- Take 5 minutes at the end of each day to manage your email inbox – organize keepers into files and delete those not required
- Name your files in methodical ways so that they are more easily recalled and found
- To recall passwords easily, pick the county in which you were born and insert a progression of numbers in the middle, for example Corn222wall, Corn333wall

SOLUTION 8
APPLY THE 80:20 RULE

The 80:20 rule is a way of defining the relationship between effort and result. One-fifth of what you do accounts for four-fifths of what you accomplish. Sadly, disorganized people devote 80 per cent of their efforts to yield only 20 per cent of their returns. Macro effort, micro result; do you identify with that feeling?

The key to effectiveness is to identify the 20 per cent of your activities that are most important, those that will yield the greatest results, and prioritize them.

In 1897, Italian economist Vilfredo Pareto described the unequal distribution of wealth in his country noting that 80 per cent of the wealth was controlled by 20 per cent of the people, a phenomenon he discovered to be consistently true throughout the world. When subsequently the 80:20 rule was applied to business and management – that 80 per cent of results come from 20 per cent of efforts – it was named after Pareto and became known as Pareto's Principle.

80:20 rule: the theory that 80 per cent of results come from 20 per cent of efforts

SOLUTION 9
GET IN THE MOOD

How much more time can you afford to waste looking for an important document? How many more opportunities can you lose out on because you missed a critical deadline? Can you really afford to wait until you are 'in the mood' to get organized? What if the desire to get organized never comes along?

with only a tiny bit of effort, you can make more progress than if you hadn't tried at all

You need to stop believing that you have to 'feel like it'. Instead, let your desire for results launch you into taking action.

SETTING A DAILY QUOTA

Although you may accomplish the most when you are 'in the mood' to organize, it is important to focus on your efforts even when you are feeling less than enthusiastic. To achieve this, set your daily quota of organizing tasks at a low level. By doing something – no matter how little – you are further ahead than if you had done nothing. You may not manage to complete a task on your first attempt, however, it's to your benefit to at least start.

QUICK FIX: TIME TO STOP
You know you have hit the wall when:
- You are just going through the motions and not making any real progress
- You start making costly errors
- Your productivity drops off
- You have completely lost track of what you are trying to achieve
- You are snappy and disagreeable to others

SOLUTION 10
GIVE YOURSELF A ROUND OF APPLAUSE

If keeping things organized doesn't come easy for you, use basic psychology to increase the probability that you'll achieve one success after another. Reward yourself as you accomplish the organizational goals you set yourself and this will incentivize you to take on more.

If you are a manager, you know how important it is to give positive reinforcement when a job has been done well. Yet the chances are that you forget to do the same with yourself.

with the right treat, even the oldest dog can learn a new trick or two

THE SELF-REWARD SYSTEM

Make the reward match the effort Larger tasks deserve bigger rewards, but a weekend break isn't appropriate for tidying your desk!

Reward yourself as soon as the job is done A trip to the cinema in three weeks' time isn't going to motivate you to get the task done right now.

Visualize the reward as you work Identifying the reward in advance will be a great boost when your energy is flagging.

The reward should support the effort Don't undermine your good work – and yes, a chocolate bar reward after exercise is counter productive.

Master the mini-reward For big tasks, implement a series of smaller rewards along the way.

ENOUGH IS ENOUGH

knowing when to stop can be just as important as knowing how to get started

Knowing when to stop is just as important as knowing how to get started on the path to becoming and remaining organized. If you're mentally or physically exhausted, and you try to induce yourself to carry on when you've had enough, you will be making it harder to pick up on the project later on. You may find yourself putting it off until next week, or maybe even next month, or even next year. So, sometimes it is critical to know when you have simply had enough.

QUICK FIX: BREAK THE TASK DOWN

Getting started on reorganizing your office can seem daunting, but not if you break the job down into smaller tasks, each to be rewarded on completion with a mini-reward. First you need to estimate how long the job will take overall, say 3 hours. Break this down into nine small rewards at 20-minute intervals, and this will motivate you to get started. Suitable rewards might be reading a few pages of your favourite magazine, having a cup of coffee, or taking a power nap. You may even find that as you get into the rhythm, you don't want to stop after 20 minutes, and that you can push yourself on to 30 or 40 minutes before breaking to take your reward.

SUMMARY: PART ONE
EMBRACING POWERFUL
PERSPECTIVES

01   **Organization can be fun** You can be more organized and getting things in order can be fun, or satisfying at the very least.

02   **Learn your organizational ABCs** Embrace the pattern of antecedent, behaviour and consequence, or the ABC of behavioural change.

03   **Bank your golden insights** Find ways to capture your ideas as these are your most valuable assets for achieving your various goals.

04   **Choose to be organized** By making a positive choice to be so, you can become and remain organized.

05   **Ask 'Who created that?'** If work, home, or any other aspect of your life is not organized, remember the likelihood is that you created the situation, and choose to take control.

06   **Live and let learn**   However disorganized you have been in the past, you can set and achieve organizational goals that might once have seemed way beyond your ability.

07   **Work smarter more of the time**   Learn to follow your inner wisdom and to rely on your instincts more routinely.

08   **Apply the 80:20 rule**   Identify the 20 per cent of your activities that yield the greatest results and prioritize them.

09   **Get in the mood**   The desire to get organized may never come along so don't waste another minute waiting for it to.

10   **Give yourself a round of applause**   Rewarding yourself as you accomplish set organizational goals will incentivize you to take on more.

NOTES

part
two

part
two

MAKING A START

SOLUTION 11
STOP MAKING EXCUSES

Even though you know it makes sense to begin a task, you find lots of reasons why you can't today. This is not uncommon. If only you could get beyond those excuses, you would be able to get started and make some headway. Having begun, the chances are that you will gain momentum, and once you see how being organized can help you to achieve the things you want to accomplish, you'll be able to continue easily.

NO MORE EXCUSES

I have been meaning to but . . . No more buts – its time to make getting organized a priority in your life. See Solution 18.

I have never been good at organizing Very few people are and even the most organized people recognize the effort required to maintain order.

I have so many other things to do And so you will for the rest of your life; getting organized will support you in the other things you 'have to do'.

Organizing will take too much time It takes less time than you think, and you should consider what disorganization is costing you.

I don't see any value in organizing You may not realize it, but many aspects of your life are already organized; you simply need to choose to extend those procedures.

I don't feel that I am accomplishing anything You will be surprised how just clearing away old papers or deleting unnecessary emails makes a difference.

I don't know how to get started A good place to start is to stop making excuses!

*break your inner resistance to
becoming more organized*

QUICK FIX: BREAKING THROUGH

If you think being disorganized is just an indication of a creative
personality – an endearing quality that colleagues are happy to
overlook – think again. Try bringing to mind the messiest person
at your workplace:

- Someone who routinely loses things
- Someone whose office is not a pleasure to visit
- Someone who is unreliable in returning borrowed items

Now that you have that person in mind, ask yourself:

- How likely is he to be picked for a team when team members
  have the option of choosing?
- How likely is he to receive a raise or promotion when others
  perform equally well and stay organized?
- How likely is he to be you?

SOLUTION 12
PRACTISE BEING IMPERFECT

'A diamond with a flaw is worth more than a pebble without imperfections.'
Chinese Proverb

Is the fear of being less than perfect stopping you from getting organized? You need to understand that sometimes just getting organized is more important than doing a perfect job.

sometimes perfect is the enemy of good enough

When briefing your staff on a task, if you give them nine or ten suggestions on how to get started, but forget one or two, they will still have plenty to get on with. Yet, if you delay organizing your team until you have every suggestion perfectly worded, you are in danger of missing the final deadline. In fact the time and effort you expend in coming up with those extra suggestions may well be unnecessary as they could do the job just as well with your original ideas.

NOBODY'S PERFECT ALL OF THE TIME

At times, striving for perfection is appropriate, yet even the most responsible of people can afford to be less than perfect and still get the job done. For example, a doctor must perform a complex operation to perfection, yet his bandaging after the operation can afford to be a little less than neat just so long as it stops the bleeding. And for an airline pilot, a landing where one wheel touches down a half second after the other will not diminish the quality of the flight.

GETTING THE JOB DONE

When you assemble data to make a decision, if you wait until you have reams of information, the opportunity in question may have passed you by. What's more, if you collect too much data you can become more confused than informed. Many decisions can be made based on instinct and intuition and still turn out fine (see Solution 7). You need only assemble the body of information necessary to help you feel comfortable with your decision, and no more than that.

> Studies have shown that the additional time spent to take a project from the 95 per cent mark to the 100 per cent mark is, in most cases, not worth it. Striving for perfection – that is ensuring the final 5 per cent is correctly done – can often take as much time as the initial 95 per cent of effort required.

QUICK FIX: GETTING MORE DONE
Look for opportunities throughout the workday when a 90 to 95 per cent effort is fine.

SOLUTION 13
BEGIN EASILY

If you have accumulated a pile of stuff that is begging to be organized, but you have trouble tackling the task, it may be because you are overcomplicating it. If you are a perfectionist you may fear that the task is going to take more time than you have: this may well be true if you plan to arrange items in the most judicious order possible, then you rearrange them again and again when you find better ones.

Relieve the pressure and increase the probability of your success by accepting this general principle: the best type of organization is the simplest.

it's time to take action when you can't tell where the mess ends and your desk begins

DEALING WITH A DISORDERLY DESK

Your desk is a disaster. You've looked at it day after day, meaning to take action, but you dread the thought of having to put everything in order. You may even be secretly hoping that a tornado will come tearing through your office today and carry everything away so that you don't have to deal with it. Yet, deep down, you know that you will benefit from getting your desk in order. So make a simple start.

FIVE SIMPLE STEPS

With just a few simple steps you can be well on your way to becoming more organized.

Step 1 Round up all the pens and pencils that populate your desk; put them in a pencil holder, can, or container.

Step 2 Grab all the Post-it pads, note pads and scraps of paper that contain any vital information, be it an address, a phone number, or a website.

Step 3 Enter the information on your hard drive or electronic planner in a folder that is designed to be a catchall for such titbits of information. Alternatively, lay down the scraps of information on to the copier to create one or two collective pages to be parked in the corner of your desk for quick reference.

Step 4 Collect all the file folders that relate to all the tasks or projects you are currently working on. Make sure each folder includes the appropriate materials, and then refile all except those you plan to work on today.

Step 5 Gather up books, reports and other large documents. Copy any relevant pages required and put in the corresponding file folder. Restack on the appropriate shelves.

QUICK FIX: IMPOSING ORDER

With any organizational task it makes for quick wins to tackle similar items all at once, then to go on to the next type of item, and the next, until order is resumed.

SOLUTION 14
GET ORGANIZED FOR LIFE'S MILESTONES

When milestone events occur in your life, embrace them as an opportunity to get organized. They can provide you with a chance to re-examine and reorganize not only your files and your furniture, but your focus on life too.

You can employ milestones as aids in your quest to become organized. Whether you are moving to a new location, a new place of employment, or a new stage in your life, make the most of these opportunities.

OPPORTUNITIES FOR REORGANIZATION

- Graduating
- Getting a new job
- Getting married
- Buying a house and relocating
- Having children
- Returning to education
- Children leaving home
- Celebrating a milestone birthday
- Going travelling
- Retiring

PLANNING AHEAD

When it comes to career aspirations, the best time to get organized is before graduation, and the more time given to planning careers or lifetime goals, the better the chance of success. Students who leave getting organized until the day after graduation may find themselves underemployed, underpaid and undervalued – or worse still unemployed and sleeping on a friend's futon. As other milestones come into view, it is just as important to plan ahead too.

when we experience
change, we have an
opportunity to change
for the better

MOVING HOME

You may move several times in your life, most likely after graduation, on getting married and to relocate for a new job. Although moving demands a high level of organization, it also provides an opportunity to make decisions about how you set up your new living space, to make choices about the sort of life you lead, and a chance for a more clutter-free, streamlined home.

Beyond the physical move itself, there's something about the moving process that facilitates order. It's a chance to re-evaluate your possessions, to decide what you value enough to retain and what can be tossed. You may decide to set up a home gym or a nursery depending on whether your focus is to get fit or to start a family. Make the most of the 'breathing space' that changes such as moving home offer you.

QUICK FIX: MOVE OFFICE

An interoffice move can give you an opportunity to set up a new work space free of all the stuff that cluttered up your old space, but that really didn't add to your productivity or peace of mind. Alternatively, you could try moving to a new desk within your department for a fresh start.

SOLUTION 15
A QUESTION OF HABIT

'Cultivate only the habits that you are willing should master you.'
Elbert Hubbard

Any time you have control over the sequence in which you tackle responsibilities, it makes sense to do those things you enjoy the least first. If you save what you like to do for last and handle the unpleasant things such as administrative tasks first, you have a greater chance of maintaining order.

It sounds so easy – so why do people resort to old, unproductive ways of approaching their day?

> *routine behaviour has far more of an impact on daily activities than you might imagine*

TIME TO CHANGE

As you get older, it is harder to change your way of doing things. Decades of habitual behaviour and habitual thought patterns all but ensure that your capacity for change in the years to come will be a fraction of what it might have been 30, 20 or even 10 years ago. But the good news is, it is never too late to change as long as you have the will to do so.

> Research shows that the more an individual engages in a particular behaviour, the stronger the neural pathways in that person's brain become. If they continue to live by habitual behaviours long enough, their ability to change will decrease significantly.

IT IS WITHIN YOUR POWER TO CHANGE

If you make yourself the promise that you will get organized starting next week, you are already setting yourself up to fail. The false promise of beginning something later is just a disguised form of procrastination, and you should not be surprised when next week turns into the beginning of next month. Before you put off taking action yet again, you should consider that:

- The energy and anxiety invested in putting off an activity can consume more energy than required to get it done
- Contemplating a change does have value, but actually doing it has more value
- The changes that you are resisting often require less effort, energy and time than you expect them to

if you're seeking to develop a new habit, the best possible time to begin is now

QUICK FIX: TAKING THE FIRST STEP

The smallest action towards getting organized can start you on the path to organizational success and is definitely preferable to taking no action at all. Take your first small step right now:

- Clear your desk
- Buy a box file
- Find a helper
- Make a list of priorities

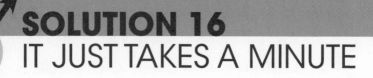

SOLUTION 16
IT JUST TAKES A MINUTE

Is your office a disaster zone? Would you like to get organized but just don't know where to begin? Do you actually dread the task? One of the most effective techniques you can use to motivate yourself to get started on any activity, organizational or otherwise, is to engage in it for just one minute at a time.

Promise yourself that you will tackle an organizing activity for a single minute. Set a timer if it helps. For just 60 seconds, straighten up whatever you can. In the course of a minute, you may only be able to tackle a very small area or handle two or three items at the most, but at the end of 60 seconds, you must honour your promise to yourself. Stop organizing and return to whatever you were doing before.

it's amazing what you can achieve in just one minute

A LITTLE AND OFTEN

This is a technique you can return to during your working day. Repeat your one-minute routine at various times later in the morning or afternoon. Each time, for just 60 seconds, organize some part of your office. It is surprising how quickly you will make progress and you will begin to feel better about yourself.

GAINING MOMENTUM

As Sir Isaac Newton proved, a body in motion tends to stay in motion, and so you will begin to find that after 60 seconds you often don't want to stop. The momentum of your efforts carries on to the next minute and the next. As this begins to happen, be supportive of yourself and let yourself 'go with the flow'. But don't be afraid to stop when you want to, if you have to, or if are too tired to carry on.

QUICK FIX: ONE MINUTE TASKS

- Clear and reorganize a desk drawer
- Straighten desktop paper overflow
- Restack a shelf
- Digest another organizing solution in this book

SOLUTION 17
WILL THE TASK BE EASIER TO HANDLE LATER ON?

When you find yourself facing a tottering pile of paperwork needing to be organized, ask yourself this key question: 'Will it be easier to handle later on?' The chances are that the answer is 'No.' Piles of paper have a tendency to grow higher, files grow thicker and stuff accumulates. In fact the mess is more likely to get worse.

Whether it's disassembling the paperwork pile, reducing the size of a bulging file, dealing with an overflowing in-tray, or managing other spaces or places at work or at home, getting organized is nearly always an easier task the sooner you take action.

about 99 times out of 100 the best time to tackle an organization task is right now

On occasion it makes sense to put a task off until later. Take for example, the mother who plans a birthday outing for her young son and his friends. Even though the family car is a mess and in desperate need of cleaning, she sensibly decides not to waste her time till after the big day. Someone is bound to spill a drink or crush a French fry into the carpet, and sweet wrappers will be stuffed between the seats. Postponing her organizing efforts for few days makes sense, and she won't have to fuss about the mess the children are making; as for the boys, they won't even notice the state of the car.

DEAL WITH THE ROADBLOCK

If you find yourself completely unable to get started on a task, you need to establish what the obstacle is.
Ask yourself:

procrastination: putting off something until a later time, either by not starting a task or not finishing one you've started

- Is the task too big for one person to handle – do you need help?
- Is lack of the right tools or equipment hampering your efforts?
- Do you lack the budget or monetary resources required to do the job?
- Is the bad weather stopping you from getting started?

Once you have identified what the problem is, you have a greater chance of dealing with it. You will also be able to identify if the reasons you give are valid or just poor excuses. For example, torrential rain is a valid reason not to tidy the garden, but a poor excuse for not organizing your office.

QUICK FIX: PROCRASTINATION BUSTERS

If you know it won't be any easier later, yet knowing so is not enough to prompt you into taking action, and you have no valid reason to put the organizing task off to another time, you may just have a problem with procrastination. You would benefit from reading *60 Second Solutions Motivation* which has great ways to tackle procrastination head-on.

SOLUTION 18
ORGANIZE ACCORDING TO YOUR PRIORITIES

To organize effectively, it helps if you identify your priorities – otherwise you're organizing without an end aim.

Priorities are often misplaced in the busy schedule of our lives. If you take the time to identify yours, you may realize that much of the clutter you have collected does not serve or support what is important to you. Understanding this will help you to free yourself of clutter more easily.

too many priorities will make you feel anxious and frustrated

THE FIVE-STEP PLAN FOR PRIORITY SETTING

You need to follow this five-step plan regularly as your priorities may change over time.

Step 1 Write down everything that is important to you or that you want to achieve; make the list as long as you like.

Step 2 Next day, revisit your list and pare it down; cross out anything that is not crucial, combine items that appear similar.

Step 3 Now restructure and redefine your list; rewrite the streamlined version. (If you're unsure if an item belongs on the list, it probably doesn't.)

Step 4 Put your list away for a couple of days, then review it as if you are seeing it for the first time; combine, drop or reword as you feel necessary.

Step 5 You are now ready to select your list of current priorities.

POWERFUL PHRASING

How you word your chosen priorities will make you more inclined to act on them, as the examples below illustrate. When writing out your priorities, always use active phrasing, i.e. start with a verb.

priorities: those things most important to a person

Passive	Active
'Money, money, money.'	'Achieve financial independence.'
'Happy job situation.'	'Strengthen my relationship with my boss.'
'Children's education'	'Provide for the education of my children.'

the organized person identifies her priorities and establishes supporting goals

QUICK FIX: KEEPING TRACK OF PRIORITIES

It is too easy to lose sight of the things we have deemed important in our fast-paced world. Simply reading your list of priorities on a regular basis is a powerful and reinforcing 'self-organizing' technique.

- Print your priorities on small cards
- Keep the printed list in your appointment book
- Keep another copy in your wallet or purse
- Retype the list into your electronic day planner
- Review periodically throughout the day, when stuck in a queue, traffic jam, or on your daily commute

SOLUTION 19
ETCH YOUR GOALS IN ALL BUT STONE

Once you have identified your priorities, setting goals will help you achieve those things that you have decided are the most important.

Aim to establish a variety of goal statements that correspond to each of the priority areas you have chosen and express them in the most positive terms possible.

EFFECTIVE GOAL SETTING

Any goal worth pursuing will need to be:

- Written down – this makes your goals difficult to ignore and easy to review
- Quantified – attaching a number to your goals makes it easier to track your progress
- Assigned a deadline – choosing a target date when a goal needs to be achieved by makes completion more likely

QUICK FIX: DAILY REMINDERS

- Write goal reinforcing statements onto Post-it notes and stick them in places you will encounter them throughout the day
- Devise statements that are uplifting and supportive such as, 'Today is going to be a great day for organizing my filing cabinet'
- Keep varying the statements otherwise it's all too easy to ignore them
- Good places to 'post' your statements include the bathroom mirror, the dashboard of your car, the refrigerator door, or by the front door
- End each day by adding an uplifting note to your diary for tomorrow

goals:
actions
that need to
be taken to
achieve your
priorities

*most people's goals are forgotten days or
weeks after they first establish them and very
few are acted on*

EFFECTIVE TECHNIQUES FOR TAKING ACTION

Set specific deadlines for goals Be clear about when you need to
complete what you set out to do – 'the middle of the week' is too
vague, 'Wednesday at 4pm' is focused.

Be positive when setting goals Avoid expressing your aims in
negative terms, so, instead of 'I will not clutter my desk for one
week', think 'I will maintain a clear, clean desk this week'.

Work with others to achieve your goals Seek out people who are
trying to achieve the same results; making yourself accountable to
others will help to motivate you to achieve your aims.

Visualize your success You are more likely to succeed if you can
picture yourself succeeding, so put those daydreams to good use.

Any goal, large or small, lends itself to the visualization
process. Simply find a quiet place where you won't be
disturbed, close your eyes, and let your imagination take
hold. See yourself accomplishing exactly what you want to
accomplish, in the way you want to accomplish it. See
yourself as organized, in control, relaxed, and ready in
ways that you know you can be.

SOLUTION 20
OWN YOUR GOALS

When you lay claim to a goal – when you make the goal yours – you are less likely to need outside intervention to achieve it. When you're willing to take responsibility for the outcome, the goal can be said to belong to you.

when you acknowledge that you can take steps to make your life more organized, your life starts to become more organized

You are well on the path to getting organized if you choose to be. So, don't wait to be told to clean up your act – make it your choice to do so.

When you were a teenager and your mother told you to clean your room, you probably did so grudgingly, dragging your feet for several hours, days or maybe even weeks before getting started. Hers was an edict that you 'had to' even though you didn't want to, and she'd nag you till you gave in. But once begun, the chances are that you began to enjoy yourself, rediscovering forgotten treasures to the music of your favourite band. Although you may not have gone about the task exactly as your mum would have, the result was the same – a more functional and organized space, if only for a short while.

HOW COMMITTED ARE YOU?

You'll find that your attitude changes once you've made a goal your own. By approaching an externally imposed task like getting organized as a personal challenge, you will begin to see it in a different light, and this will make it far easier to accomplish.

If the job you have been given to do is not one of your choosing, find ways in which you can engage in shaping the goal to make the task more enjoyable and rewarding for yourself. Say, for example, you have to complete the entire store inventory by the end of the month: tackle the job one aisle at a time or begin with all of the high-priced items first – the choice is yours.

sometimes resistance is futile, but even the most mundane task can be enjoyed if you make it your own

QUICK FIX: OWING AN ORGANIZATIONAL TASK

Before getting started, take a few moments to ask yourself:

- What is involved?
- What can I bring to the assignment?
- What will I do first?
- How will I take charge?
- How will I feel when the task is completed?
- Is it really worth making such a fuss about?

SUMMARY: PART TWO
MAKING A START

11   **Stop making excuses**   Once you begin to see how being organized can help you to achieve the things you want to accomplish, you'll be able to continue easily.

12   **Practise being imperfect**   Sometimes just getting organized to take on a task is more important than doing a perfect job.

13   **Begin easily**   You will increase your chances of success if you accept the general principle that the best type of organization is the simplest.

14   **Get organized for life's milestones**   Embrace life's milestones as opportunities to re-examine and reorganize your files, your furniture and your focus on life.

15   **A question of habit**   Make a change for the better and don't resort to old, unproductive ways of approaching your day.

16 It just takes a minute One of the most effective techniques you can use to motivate yourself to get started on any activity is to engage in it for just one minute at a time.

17 Will the task be easier to handle later on? Create a personal incentive to deal with the organizational task now, whether you feel in the mood or not.

18 Organize according to your priorities To organize effectively, you need to identify your priorities – otherwise you're organizing without an end aim.

19 Etch your goals in all but stone Setting goals will help you to achieve your priorities.

20 Own your goals Don't wait to be told to get more organized – make it your choice to do so.

NOTES

part
three

part
three

LISTING AND CHARTING YOUR WAY

SOLUTION 21
BECOME YOUR OWN MANAGEMENT TOOL

A management pitfall, particularly in recent years, is to rely on sophisticated scheduling tools as if they were the be-all and end-all. But for any of these to be effective, the information that they hold must be kept up to date, and that comes back down to you.

There is no escaping it: you are the most important tool in organizing your schedule, your time and your entire life.

EFFECTIVE MANAGEMENT TOOLS

That is not to say that you cannot make use of the wide range of scheduling tools on offer. Indeed, it makes sense to use palmtop organizers, electronic calendars, time management software, day planners, and so on, if such tools:

- Support the way you live and work
- Are simple and convenient for you to use
- Are easy for you to keep current

all tools you use to manage your time, from simple to-do lists to complicated scheduling software, require continual input and updates

IT ALL COMES DOWN TO YOU

Unless you 'feed' the system, these tools will very quickly fail to reflect the current tasks and responsibilities you face. With any planning or scheduling tool, someone has to be in the driver's seat. If you're not keeping up with the timelines you have established, particularly if you are relying on a scheduler in coordination with others, it will quickly become ineffectual. Likewise, if you take on more than you can cope with, planning and scheduling tools may alert you to what you have done, but it is up to you to get back on track.

the most critical factor in organizing, planning and scheduling your time is you

QUICK FIX: KEEPING MENTALLY ALERT

The mental energy you bring to maintaining your organizing system is what fuels your efforts. A clear mind is a fundamental step on the path to a clear desk and an organized life so here are a few ideas to 'wake you up' throughout the day.

- Spray your office with an energizing aroma
- Go for a power walk at lunchtime
- Replace a chocolate-bar snack with a banana on an oatcake
- Drink plenty of water – at least 2 litres – each day
- Do nothing at all but stare out the window for a couple of minutes

SOLUTION 22
SCHEDULE TIME TO ORGANIZE

'The definition of insanity is doing the same thing over and over and expecting a different result.'
Benjamin Franklin

The first step to being organized is making time to be so. You need to schedule some organizing tasks into your diary just as you would any other important obligation.

Scheduling organizing time increases the chance that you will actually engage in essential organizing activities. By formally scheduling sessions for organizing, you are automatically raising the task to the status of an important commitment.

MAKE TIME TODAY

Many people feel as if organizational tasks intrude upon all the other 'important' things scheduled in their day. But they fail to realize how being disorganized can cost them time and mental energy.

You know it's time to schedule your first organizing slot when:

- You spend 5 minutes or more looking for a document
- Month-old papers clutter up your desk
- You have trouble finding an item you use frequently
- You have a wall of unread magazines and journals
- You have hundreds of emails accumulating in your inbox
- You can't open your drawers because they are so full of stuff

deadline:
a time limit for
any activity

*by scheduling organizing sessions
on your calendar you elevate the
importance of the task*

Allot a 45-minute session and give your full attention to the task for that block of time. If, at the end of the session you've not finished, just schedule another slot.

THE POWER OF DEADLINES

Many people dread deadlines. They regard them as restrictions imposed upon them that routinely foster stress and anxiety; but looked at another way, deadlines can serve as powerful motivators toward the accomplishment of our goals.

Harnessing the power of deadlines in your schedule can help you to accomplish your objectives. Consider what deadlines you can impose on yourself to increase the probability of completing your organizing goals. And, if the organizing task ahead seems too daunting, break it down into a series of tasks, each to be achieved one at a time before moving on to the next. Say, for example, you set yourself the deadline of clearing your desk by the end of the week; if the desk has four drawers, clear one each day, and the desktop on the final day.

SOLUTION 23
BALANCE TODAY'S TASKS VERSUS TOMORROW'S

Everyone should use some kind of list as an organizing tool for getting things done. If you already maintain a to-do list, you can use it more effectively to support your priorities by strategically lengthening it without overloading yourself.

By managing a super-long-to-do list – a list of absolutely everything you need to do to achieve your aims – you'll have a clear idea of what you face all in one place keeping you focused on your priorities for years to come.

the trick is to balance the short-term tasks and activities against the long-term ones

MAKING YOUR LIST

Step 1 Write down everything you need to do to achieve your life's priorities (see Solution 18) – at this stage don't worry about following an order or that the list stretches to several pages.

Step 2 Review your list and move those tasks that need to be accomplished in the short term – those things you need to do this week – to the front page.

Step 3 Arrange the remaining tasks into medium to long-term activities.

Step 4 Review and update your lists on a weekly basis, continually drawing from the backlist to move items to your front page as they become necessary to action.

Step 5 Schedule your front-page list into your diary each week.

A FEW DOS AND DON'TS

Do keep your dynamic to-do list – things to achieve in the short term – to a single page.

Do remember to review and update your list on a regular basis.

Do use the long to-do list method to help you manage long-term projects as well as your life's priorities.

Don't be tempted to carry over tasks to the next day or procrastination will take hold.

Don't reserve your list for only vital, glamorous activities – everyday chores are just as important.

Don't forget to list recurring tasks, particularly those easy to put off, organizational tasks.

To save both time and money, it makes sense to maintain the things we value. For example, taking your car for a regular service means it is less likely to break down.

Also, by eating sensibly, taking regular exercise, and having regular medical check ups we can increase our chances of living a long, healthy life. So too, when it comes to the continuing challenge of staying organized, your to-do list needs to be developed with a 'preventative maintenance' approach. Listing organizing tasks on your to-do list will, in the long term, save you time, money and effort, and avert many mini-crises.

SOLUTION 24
CREATE A CLARIFYING CHECK LIST

In today's busy world, it's easy to lose sight of what we want to accomplish when we constantly have too much to do. Preparing a to-do list can help us to focus, but to be truly effective a to-do list, which is often hastily composed with the items listed in no particular order, must be polished into a check list.

Keeping a check list – a comprehensive list of important or relevant actions to be taken in a specific order – will help you to work most effectively.

CREATING A CHECK LIST

A check list can have fewer than three items or more than nine, but for practical purposes a list usually works best within these limits – too short and it's not really a list, too long and it is overwhelming. So, pick one organizing task that needs immediate attention, and write your check list.

- Create a to-do list of between three to nine steps
- Order the list in action order – what must be done first, what must be done second, and so on
- Review and refine your list – change the order, combine or divide tasks, elaborate as necessary
- Tackle the items in the order that you have listed them and make sure each is completed before moving on to the next
- If a task cannot be completed, take it as far as you can, then move on to the next one, and so on until the list is completed

AN ORGANIZATIONAL CHECK LIST

If your challenge is to reclaim control of your department's resource library, here's what your check list might look like:

1 Clear the entire room
2 Dust the centre table
3 Dust and clean the shelves
4 Evaluate the documents taken from the shelves
5 Bin what is outdated, re-shelve what is relevant
6 Invite someone to witness the results of your efforts

QUICK FIX: THE PRAISE PRINCIPLE

When you receive praise for your efforts, the positive reinforcement increases the probability that you will extend your organizational efforts to other places at work and at home too. So show your colleagues or your boss the results of your efforts, and if they are less than effusive, applaud yourself.

SOLUTION 25
MAP YOUR WAY

Some people find preparing a to-do list just too difficult. The good news is that for those of you who are visually oriented there is another way. You can use a mind map – a graphics orientated technique to capture your ideas for approaching any task set yourself.

First you must describe the task in a brief, simple phrase, write it in the centre of a piece of paper and circle it. Then, working from this core circle outwards, draw arrowed lines to represent the ideas that you have. From these lines, other ideas will 'branch' out as they occur to you, ensuring that all the ideas you have are 'captured' in one place.

STARTING A MIND MAP

If you are a new employee seeking to become more knowledgeable about your company's top customers, your core task might be 'Research the top customers'. Write the idea in the middle of the page and circle it. The first arrowed line from the core idea might point to a second phrase, 'List the five top customers'.

From there, you might have options as to how to gather data, what sources to tap, and how to store what you find, each of which could merit its own arrow. If it helps, write the name of each information source at the end of an arrow.

mind map:
a diagram used to represent words, ideas, tasks, or other items linked to and arranged around a central key word or idea

GET CREATIVE

Once a trail is completed, return to your central task (in the middle of the page) and start another one. So to 'Research the top customers' you may start a line extending from that core task that reads, 'Obtain online materials', and branching off from this trail, arrowed lines to 'Consult the company's customer database', or 'Websurf for information', and branching out from these, 'Acquire hard-copy brochures, literature, and catalogues'. Each time a thought occurs additional lines with additional arrows should point to these adjacent tasks.

Soon your page will start to fill. Beginning in the centre and branching out in many different directions, you create a visual map of the key activities and tasks involved in organizing and executing your 'Research the top customers' campaign.

Some people find it helpful to use coloured pens or highlighters to stimulate creativity and make the page more visually pleasing. The key is to let the 'sparks fly' as you create your visual map. How you plot your ideas is completely up to you: use boxes, little squares, stars, or any other symbol you choose to; connect tasks by broken lines, dotted lines, double lines, or squiggly lines. Whatever works for you.

when your map is complete start using it as your trail guide

SOLUTION 26
CHART YOUR COURSE

There are so many devices on the market today that it is possible to take your office with you wherever you go. You can maintain your database of contacts, send faxes, keep up with email, and log on to the Internet wherever you are in the world.

Yet, whether you choose to use sophisticated project management and scheduling software on your computer, electronic organizer or mobile phone, or you prefer to use non-technical tools such as hand-drawn charts or grids, the underlying components of effectively organizing your day while making progress on selected tasks and projects remain the same. Any goal that you intend to achieve needs to be written down, quantified and assigned a specific time frame.

if you don't have a timeline attached to a task or project, then 'any time' will do, and 'never' is the likely result

PLOTTING YOUR STEPS

Carefully plotting your steps along the way to reaching your goals is more likely to result in:

- Significant increase in your chances of accomplishment
- Greater productivity
- Effective time management
- Less stress and anxiety

SOME SIMPLE TRUTHS

More powerful, feature-laden scheduling software, calendar systems, and other project organizers become available with each passing month. But no matter how sophisticated the technology you use, there are a few simple truths you would do well to remember.

Garbage in yields garbage out There is no benefit to you if the information you are adding is not current or is inaccurate (see Solution 21).

Nothing in yields nothing out Essential to remember when using any scheduling or organizing tools.

A fool and his money are easily parted The latest iPhone may look snazzy, but it will be of no use if you don't know how to access and update your information.

QUICK FIX: LEARN MORE

There are three basic forms of project management and/or scheduling tools:

- Milestone charts (see Solutions 27 and 28)
- Flow charts (see Solution 29)
- Calendars (see Solution 30)

SOLUTION 27
PLOT YOUR PATH

A milestone chart, formally known as a Gantt chart after originator Henry L Gantt, is a project control chart that provides a graphic schedule for the planning and controlling of work, and recording progress towards stages of a project.

A SIMPLE MILESTONE CHART

This example of a milestone chart gives a quick view of progress on several tasks in relation to time.

	Month 1	Month 2	Month 3	Month 4	Month 5
Task 1	>>>>>>>>>>>>>>>>>>				
Task 2		>>>>>>>>>>>>>>>>>>>>>>>>>>			
Task 3			>>>>>>>>>>>>>>>>		
Task 4				>>>>>>>>>>	

Henry L Gantt worked as a management consultant, but his background was in mechanical engineering, and his self-named easily viewed scheduling and monitoring diagram was founded on his ship building work during WWI. Gantt charts were subsequently used to schedule and monitor large construction projects including the Hoover Dam started in1931.

CREATING A MILESTONE CHART

Suppose one of your priorities is to advance in your career. One of your goals in support of that priority is to achieve a raise of £4,000 at the end of year review appraisal scheduled in 11 weeks. To reach that goal, you've identified five tasks that will greatly enhance the value of your services to your bosses. These are:

- Rewriting the orientation manual for new employees
- Getting an article published in one of the top three magazines in your industry
- Starting an online newsletter for your top clients and prospects
- Completing an assigned report three weeks before it's due date
- Participating at the key trade show by making important contacts to gather critical information for your boss

By using a more sophisticated version of the milestone chart you can plan out how to allocate your time and resources to complete each of the tasks in the time you have available. Your first job is to plot the most basic information for each task as shown below. Then you will move on to add sub tasks under each task area as explained in Solution 28.

Weeks

Task	1	2	3	4	5	6	7	8	9	10	11
Rewrite manual	>>>>>>>>>>>>										
Publish article		>>>>>>			>>>		>>>				
Online zine				>>>>>>>>>>>>>>>>>>>>>>>>							
DEF report					>>>>>>>>>						
Trade show							>>>				

SOLUTION 28
DIG DEEPER WITH A MILESTONE CHART

Once you have plotted each task that you need to achieve on to your milestone chart, you can move on to add sub tasks under each. Depending on how much detail you require, you may have anywhere from three to 15 sub tasks in support of a given task.

How much detail you choose to outline is completely up to you. The important thing is that what you record is of value to you and assists you in your progress towards your chosen goals.

PLANNING SUB TASKS

Take, for example, the task 'Publish article', to achieve this you may first have to interview some people or conduct some research; you will have to organize your notes and create an outline, before writing a first draft; after asking a colleague to review the article, you may need to allow time to write a second draft, before submitting the final version to the publishers. An example of what your chart may now look like is given on the opposite page.

milestone chart: a visual plotting tool to give a clear indication of both the timeline and sequencing of tasks in support of your overall goals

MAKING MILESTONE CHARTS WORK FOR YOU

- List the level of detail that works for you; avoid over complication
- Use a broken line symbol to denote germination time
- Place left and right arrows to indicate distinct periods of activity
- Insert blanks when no activity is planned
- Add initials to indicate a colleague's cooperation or when delegation is required
- Include footnotes if useful

QUICK FIX: CLEAR INFORMATION

Use colour to indicate your progress at a glance:

Green	To denote the start of a task
Yellow	To indicate a critical function
Blue	To represent completion

Weeks

Task	1	2	3	4	5	6	7	8	9	10	11
Rewrite manual	>>>	>>>>	>>>>>								
Publish article		>>>	>>>>>	>>>>>	>>>>>	>>>>>	>>>>>	>>>>>	>>>>>	>>>>>	>
Interviews		>>									
Research			>>								
Organize			>								
Outline				>>							
1st draft					>>						
Peer review						>>					
2nd draft							>>				
Submit								>			
Follow up											>
Online zine					>>>	>>>>	>>>>>	>>>>>	>>>>>		
DEF report					>>>	>>>>>	>>>				
Trade show							>>>	>			

SOLUTION 29
GO WITH THE FLOW

A flow chart is a simple device to enable you to convey information, particularly relating to processes, in a step-by-step flow.

Generally most flow charts are made up of three main types of symbol: elongated circles, which signify the start or end of a process; rectangles, which show instructions or actions; and diamonds, which show decisions that must be made. These symbols are connected one to the other by arrows, showing the flow of the process.

By breaking processes and tasks down in this way, you can concentrate more intently on each individual step without being overwhelmed by the bigger picture.

erasable charts can be bought – a valuable feature for making course corrections

FLOWING BY

While flow charts are widely used to convey a process (how something happens), they are also convenient for helping you to:

- Track project progress
- Stay on target
- Accomplish your goals and stay organized

FLOW CHART FACTS

Multi-resource projects You can plot activities related to a task or project area where many different people or resources may be required.

Contingency planning You can look at several possible outcomes – if the answer to a question is yes, the flow chart proceeds along one path, and if the answer is no, it proceeds along another.

Feedback loops If, for example, an article is submitted to a publication and the editor wants specific changes, the feedback loop could encompass where you go next.

Effective communication As with milestone charts, different colours, shapes and symbols can be used to convey different types of information at a glance.

Keeping to schedule If your flow chart extends to the right rather than downwards, a timeline can be added to the top or bottom of the chart.

flow chart: a simple diagram that maps out a process for easy communication

QUICK FIX: KEEP IT SIMPLE

The main purpose of flow charts is to communicate information. Be warned, if you use too many obscure symbols, there's a good chance that you will fail in this aim. It is best to keep things simple. It may help to add a key at the bottom of the chart to show exactly what each symbol and colour represents.

SOLUTION 30
STAY ON TRACK

For goals that stretch on for weeks, months, years or even decades, starting with the end in mind is the only practical way to proceed. In addition to milestone charts and flow charts, wall calendars can be another effective way to keep on track.

using a calendar to ensure progress toward chosen goals is a good way to stay organized

THE 'BLOCK-BACK' METHOD

Let's take a simple example – planning and monitoring a project that must be initiated and completed in the same calendar month. The goal is to prepare a new orientation manual for new employees. The due date is 30 March. So, on 30 March 'Complete manual' is written (see calendar opposite).

Working from the end date back, the project is broken down into tasks that need to take place before the manual can be delivered. If higher management input is required, a conference must be arranged to brief department heads and obtain their input. This is scheduled for 22 March. Likewise, the project manager determines what needs to happen before the conference, and in each case, dates are plotted on the calendar.

With this method it is easy to see that if any interim dates are missed successful completion of the project may be jeopardized. So, each interim date represents a mini-deadline. Hence, the block back method is a built-in system for ensuring a project continues according to plan.

March

Sunday	Monday	Tuesday	Wednesday	Thursday	Friday	Saturday
	1	2	3	4	5	6
7	8	9 *Initiate review*	10	11	12	13
14	15 *Proofread manual*	16	17	18	19 *Assemble copies*	20
21	22 *Schedule conference*	23	24	25	26	27
28	29	30 *Complete manual*				

with its interim mini-deadlines, the block-back method has a built-in system for keeping to plan

QUICK FIX: WALL CALENDAR

You could use actual calendar pages from the current year for however many months are relevant to the project you are managing, and post the calendar pages on the wall so that the information is always on view.

SUMMARY: PART THREE
LISTING AND CHARTING
YOUR WAY

21   **Become your own management tool** The most important tool in organizing your schedule, your time and your life is you.

22   **Schedule time to organize** By formally scheduling sessions for organizing, you automatically raise the task to the status of an important commitment.

23   **Balance today's tasks versus tomorrow's** Everyone should use a list as an organizing tool for getting things done.

24   **Create a clarifying check list** A comprehensive list of important or relevant actions to be taken in a specific order will help you to work most effectively.

25   **Map your way** Use a mind map – a graphics orientated technique to capture your ideas – for approaching any task you set yourself.

26 **Chart your course** Find ways to carefully plot your steps along the way to reaching your goals if you want to be successful.

27 **Plot your path** A milestone chart – a project control chart providing a graphic schedule for the planning of work – can help you record progress towards stages of a project.

28 **Dig deeper with a milestone chart** Use a milestone chart to outline all the information that is of value to you to help you to achieve your chosen goals.

29 **Go with the flow** A flow chart can help you to convey information, particularly relating to processes, in a simple step-by-step flow that is easy to understand.

30 **Stay on track** Working backwards from your due date with the block-back calendar method may be best for long-term projects.

NOTES

part

four

part
four

RECLAIMING YOUR PLACES AND SPACES

SOLUTION 31
PRETEND IT'S YOUR FIRST DAY

When your work space becomes too disorganized, rearrange the area completely from scratch. This highly viable strategy works particularly well with the surface of your desk.

Think back to your first day. No doubt, when you approached your office or cubicle, your desk, filing cabinets, shelves, and other spaces had been de-cluttered of your predecessor's belongings to make room for yours.

Imagine that you are sitting down at your desk for the first time. Would you continue to keep the items that are currently on it and, if so, would they be placed in their current locations? If not, now's the time to do something about it.

THE ERGONOMIC DESK

The configuration of your desktop should suit the way you work and operate. If you adopt the 'Day One' mindset, your rearranged desk may boost your productivity and your enjoyment of your work space. Consider the following:

- Should items be moved to the right or left? (If you're left-handed, consider the times you reach across to the right side for something.)
- Should items be closer or further away? (Having some items at arm's length may give you a chance for a stretch throughout the day.)
- Can tools be rearranged for economy of motion?
- Should anything be removed from the desktop?
- Should anything be added?

THE EFFECTIVE WORK SPACE

What, precisely, do you need to have on your desktop? The simple answer is, anything you use on a recurring and daily basis. Items listed below need to be close at hand, but are they are best stored in a drawer within your desk, or possibly on a table or credenza behind you. For more on defeating desk clutter, see Solution 32.

- Paper
- Letterhead
- Business envelopes
- Letter opener
- Stamps
- Ruler
- Stapler and staple remover
- Scissors
- Business cards
- Drawer dividers
- Tissues
- Pens, pencils, highlighters and felt-tip pens
- Markers
- Post-it pads
- Paper clips

---

anything you can't use on a daily or recurring basis does not belong in your desk

---

QUICK FIX: KEEPING IT CLEAR

It is okay to have personal objects such as pictures, plants and personal motivators at work. In fact, if an item enhances your productivity, efficiency and creativity, it is a valuable asset. But you should place these near and not on your desk.

SOLUTION 32
DEFEAT DESK CLUTTER

When you begin each day with a clear, organized desk and a clean, organized office, you will work with more energy, focus, direction and motivation. It is easier to concentrate on those tasks that you deem most important and urgent when your work space is clear of clutter.

Your aim should be to clear your desk and surrounding area at the end of each work day.

effective management of the desk surface is one of the most key indicators of the organized individual

REAP THE BENEFITS

Clearing your desk and surroundings each evening requires discipline. After a full day at work, most people just want to go home. However, when you arrange your materials in the evening for higher productivity the next day, a host of benefits come into play.

More satisfaction When you leave with a clear desk, you give yourself a sense of completion.

More energy When you arrive in the morning and find yourself greeted by neat, clean surroundings, you gain a boost.

More direction With no unfinished business on your desk from the night before, you will be able to focus on what you want to accomplish today.

More motivation For ongoing projects it can be prudent to leave one file open on your desk to catch your attention first thing tomorrow.

THE DISEMBARKATION ZONE

Your goal at all times is to have as much open space as possible to support the way you work. You want clear, clean, flat surfaces, a place where you can open packages and break down the mail, thereby diminishing piles and accumulations as you work.

do not fall into the habit of leaving unfinished piles of work on your desk each night

Inside your desk retain items that you use on a weekly basis. Recognize, however, that your desk drawers are not for storing supplies. The guiding principle is to have an item inside your desk if and when you periodically need it. Keep extra supplies in a file folder, a storage locker, or in some other space away from the epicentre of your creative and productive post.

Only use a desk drawer to contain file folders that represent current projects. All other files should be kept in a filing cabinet.

QUICK FIX: HANDS FREE

Long-life stampers, which can be printed with 'Draft' or 'Review and Return,' help reduce the time you spend writing by hand when organizing and sending out materials.

SOLUTION 33
SHOW YOUR SHELVES WHO'S BOSS

If your office shelves are crammed full and on the verge of collapse, the problem is likely to be that you are storing items on them that should not be there.

It is fine to use shelves to temporarily store materials but not on a long-term basis. It's very easy to lose track of this. Once a temporary pile becomes a semi-permanent file, you begin to lose control of what you're retaining, and the clutter starts to mount.

SHELVE OR FILE?

The issue of what to house on your shelves versus what is best contained in a filing cabinet is relatively easy to address. Essentially, shelves are best used to do the following:

- Temporarily store items you are likely to use within 10–15 days
- Store items that are too large to fit in a filing cabinet
- Keep a collection together, such as 12 issues of the same magazine in an upright storage box
- Provide a temporary home for projects in progress
- Store books, directories, supply catalogues and other items with spine labels

You can temporarily park materials for a project-in-progress on your shelves so that you can keep a clear desk. The project materials should rotate from your desk to the shelf and back to your desk as required, but as the project progresses the materials pile should be getting thinner, and eventually be removed from your shelves altogether.

THE SUPPLY CABINET

Supply cabinets are designed to house items in bulk. While you should strive to arrange items on your shelves with precision, supply cabinets allow for more leeway. However, you should be able to open a supply cabinet and readily find what you need.

If you work in an office, it could be someone else's responsibility to maintain the supply cabinet but each employee should follow the basic etiquette:

- All like items should be kept together
- When returning surplus items from desk to supplies cabinet, put them in their allocated space
- If the last of an item is taken, throw away the box and let the person who orders the stationery supplies know

QUICK FIX: TOSS IT

If you don't need some item or haven't looked at it since the day you acquired it, it is probably not worth filing or storing. Be brave and resist the urge to keep it to satisfy the 'I know the moment I toss it I'll need it' syndrome. Remember, in the digital office:

- Nearly any list, report, or document can be replaced
- Somebody else will have a copy
- It's probably on the Internet
- It's probably on somebody's hard drive

SOLUTION 34
GAIN POWER OVER PAPER

In an article in 1975, *Business Week* magazine confidently predicted that the office of the future would be a paperless one, yet today it is estimated that over 2.5 trillion pages are printed off our computers each year, and that figure is expected to grow over the next decade.

> UK offices print up to 120 billion pieces of paper annually, the equivalent of a paper mountain more than 8,000 miles high

In fact if you analyzed your most repetitive task, it is highly likely that handling paper would top the list most days. So to get better organized, you need to better manage your own personal paper mountain.

Once you have your paperwork in order you will find yourself freed from all clutter that usually surrounds you so that you can focus on creative, fulfilling, more productive work.

THE PAPER CHALLENGE

Your mission is to whittle down all those pages of catalogues, magazines, reports, letters, and any other paper materials that come your way so that you retain only that which can be useful to you. It can help to ask yourself a series of questions to quickly determine what to do with the next item that crosses your desk:

- What does this document represent?
- Is there any reason to retain this?
- Who else needs to know about this?

**paperless
office:**
an environment in
which the use of
paper is eliminated
or greatly
reduced

FOUR STEPS TO PROCESS PAPER EFFECTIVELY

Use this simple four-step process to assess
what to do with the material you receive
every day:

Step 1 Act on it.
Step 2 Delegate it.
Step 3 File it.
Step 4 Recycle it.

Aim to keep your 'act on it' file as thin as possible, and
organize the items in it according to priority, with what's
important and urgent on top, moving through to what is
unimportant and not urgent at the bottom of the pile.

QUICK FIX: THE JUNK DRAWER

Although desirable, it is not always possible to deal with printed
materials as you receive them, for example, when you're in the middle
of an important project and have a deadline to meet. Dedicate a
drawer (or box) as a holding space for those times when you simply
'can't deal with that right now'. But always make time before you
leave the office each day to open your junk drawer and apply the
four-step process.

SOLUTION 35
SMILE WHILE YOU FILE

When you file items intelligently, you enable yourself to efficiently retrieve what you need when you need it. There is no doubt about it, this is a discipline; but the good news is, it is one you can learn.

80 per cent of what most people file is never used again

GETTING STARTED

If it's been some time since you organized your filing cabinet, get started by tackling just half a drawer each week.

Step 1 Assemble the tools you'll need to be effective, such as blank file folders, file folder labels, markers, colour-coded dots, a stapler, paper clips, fasteners, and Post-it notes.

Step 2 Grab the first file and examine its contents. Ask yourself: What can be combined? What needs to be re-allocated? What can be thrown away?

Step 3 Repeat for the second, third, fourth file in the drawer, etc, until half a drawer is complete.

Step 4 Schedule time next week to tackle the second half of the drawer.

As Jim Cathcart, author of *The Acorn Principle*, says, 'Filing is not about storing, it is about retrieval.' You file things because either they will help you to be prosperous in the future (the information you retain has power), or because there are penalties for not filing (you won't be able to complete your taxes). All items that you file should have some potential future value.

SECRETS TO FILING SUCCESS

Think small Keep your files contained within a two-drawer filing cabinet.

Be colourful Use coloured file folders for different types of information: green for finances, blue for career progression, yellow for taxes, and so on.

Fewer files, more in them Seek to have fewer large files of like items as opposed to a larger number of smaller files – you'll find it quicker to locate what you need if there are fewer choices to begin with.

Pare it down Routinely discard extraneous information and be on the lookout for opportunities to reduce the paper piles.

Prioritize the file's contents Place important and urgent materials at the front and least important and least urgent materials at the back.

Creative labelling The labels you place on the tab section of each file folder largely governs what you file and how you file it. As well as general headings such as 'Office Supplies' or 'Personal Documents', headings such as 'Review Year End' or 'Hold Until After the Merger' may be a useful.

QUICK FIX: DON'T KNOW WHERE TO FILE

Start a file labelled 'Don't Know Where to File' to make a home for the handful of things that your instincts tell you to retain but which don't fit in with anything else you are working on at the moment. To stop the file from growing too large, review monthly and act on, delegate, refile or toss.

SOLUTION 36
TICKLE YOUR FANCY WITH TICKLER FILES

Tickler files – also referred to as suspended or follow-on files – enable you to hold on to information for review at a later date.

By setting a date when you're going to review material in the future, you can find a home for much of the stuff that clutters your desk, your office and your mind. You are simply placing the information in a location where you'll be able to retrieve it at a time when it makes the most sense to deal with them.

SETTING UP CALENDAR TICKLER FILES

First you need to set up a daily and monthly 'rotating tickler file'. Begin by setting up a file folder for each month of the year, January to December. Now set up an additional 31 file folders marked 1 to 31 (for the maximum days of the month). These 43 file folders, 1 to 31 and January to December, allow you to park information in the appropriate place when the item doesn't have to be dealt with right now. Keep the number files at the front of the pack, followed by the forthcoming month, with the remaining months of the year in order at the back of the pack.

SOME EXAMPLE OF USING TICKLER FILES

- If information is put into your in-tray in March, looks interesting, but doesn't need to be acted on until 25 April, put it in the April file folder
- At the beginning of April, open up the April file folder, take out all the contents, and allocate the items to file folders 1 to 31 as appropriate and replace the April file folder at the back of the pack

- If you receive something on the 3 April, but don't have to deal with it until 18 April, put it in the file folder two to three days before the due date
- Review your tickler files at the start of each week, and perhaps one or two more times during the week

PRE-EMPTIVE FILE FOLDERS

As a useful variation on the tickler file system, you can create file folders based on the priorities you have identified and the goals you have established in support of those priorities. Creating file folders in advance of having anything to put into them affirms the goals you have chosen and might include:

- Insurance plans
- Equipment acquisition
- Benefits packages
- Holiday to Bali
- Digital cameras
- Grants and awards

QUICK FIX: ELECTRONIC 'TICKLERS'

You can also set up reminders by employing the calendar function in your computer program. This helps you to stay on top of important projects, meet deadlines, and post birthday cards and gifts in plenty of time.

SOLUTION 37
GET CLUTTER-BUSTING

When piles of clutter threaten to take over your space at home or at work it is time to take decisive action. First, gather together all the tools you will need, including file folders, rubber bands, paper clips, staplers, boxes, rubbish bags, and so on. Give yourself a set amount of time – no less than 15 minutes and no more than 30 – to go through each pile to assess what might best be done with each item in it.

You have just four options when confronting what to do with stuff – act on it, delegate it, file it, or recycle/toss it.

whittle out the unnecessary and deal with the rest

THE LAW OF DIMINISHING RETURNS

Be decisive and place each item in either the 'act on it' pile, 'delegate it' pile, 'file it' pile, or 'recycle/toss it' pile. Make a quick assessment and go on to the next. Once complete, deal with the 'act on it' pile first. Rank the items according to their importance and urgency.

- If an item is both important and urgent, put it at the top of the pile
- If an item is important but not urgent, place it next
- If an item is urgent, place it after that
- If an item is neither urgent nor important, recycle, file or delegate it

TACKLE THE MOST IMPORTANT ITEMS FIRST

Always tackle the most important and urgent items first. If you find that you have several of these, apply the prioritizing process once more. Make an estimate of how long it will take to complete each item, add together and multiply by 1.5 (things often take longer than we expect). Then marshal your resources. If there is too much to do yourself, see if anyone can help you.

Work on item1 to completion (or as far as you can take it if you have to wait for someone else's input), then proceed to item 2, and so on until all are complete. If you feel your energy sapping, it is okay to turn your attention to items of lesser significance that don't require as much mental effort. But when you feel ready, do return to the most important items, which are still situated conveniently on the top of the pile.

QUICK FIX: ELECTRONIC CLUTTER

For dealing with clutter on your hard drive, a variety of software programs are available, such as Time Saver Wolf at *www.lonewolf-software.com*, which allows users to prioritize information. This software offers a 'category tree' system that allows you to create, edit, rename and move categories as you wish.

SOLUTION 38
PARE DOWN AND PERSEVERE

'Happiness is a place between too little and too much.'
Finnish proverb

When you pare down, you increase the probability of succeeding in your quest to be organized. While merely reducing the volume of paper confronting you won't solve all your organizational challenges, it will certainly have many benefits. A slimmer file is easier to carry; fewer notes in front of you mean fewer notes to digest; more focused research materials cuts down on reading time.

the less you have, the easier it is to find what you have chosen to retain

The truth is, too much information can bring on feelings of frustration and anxiety. So it is in your interest to be continually on the lookout for ways to pare down your accumulations.

Kaizen, meaning continuous improvement, is an essential part of a Japanese philosophy about how to approach work. The seasoned kaizen practitioner seeks ways to make improvements that offer the most immediate and dramatic paybacks. Such results prompt one to look for even more ways to improve. The art of seeking continuous improvement is challenging but fun. Consider in what ways each and every day you can continually improve the organization of your spaces at work and at home.

DO YOU NEED IT?

By whittling away what you no longer need you will physically have the space, both within your desk and filing cabinets and on your hard drive, to accommodate the new information that is on its way. Consider what you can dispense with.

Item	Toss or recycle if ...	Retain if ...
Business cards	You can't recall the person, or the goods or services provided	You have a cardholder, can scan them, know or feel you will use them
Papers, files, and documents	Old, outdated, or uninformative; have been transferred to disk	Your duty to retain; refer to often; has future value
Reports, magazines	Old, outdated, stacking up	Vital to your career or wellbeing
Books, guides, directories	Notes have been made or key pages copied or scanned; obsolete or been updated	Part of a collection; referred to often; has sentimental value; you want to
CDs, DVDs, videos, cassettes	You never play, or you can take it or leave it, or plays poorly	You play it, you like it, you couldn't bear to part with it. It's a keepsake
Mementos, memorabilia	No longer holds meaning or you have many similar items; you do not have room; you've moved on	Still evokes strong memories; looks good on display
Gifts, cards, presents	Never used and not wanted; the giver need never know	Often used; glad you have it; saving for a special reason

SOLUTION 39
SLOW THE PAPER CHASE

When you make a purchase by mail, your name is sold and circulated to dozens of catalogue houses. Some organizations repeatedly send huge amounts of junk mail, which wastes your time and clutters up your life.

If your name gets into the direct mailing list system, you may be bombarded with paper in direct contradiction to your desire to pare down, simplify your life and stay in control. But it is within your power to fight back.

BEATING THE JUNK MAILERS

Here are a few ways to help you to stay off mailing lists in the first place:

- When making a mail order purchase, include a pre-printed label that reads, 'I don't want my name placed on any mailing lists whatsoever, and forbid the use, sale, rental, or transfer of my name'
- When shopping online, look out for similar wording on the website and remember to check the box; look carefully as it is often hard to find or in a smaller font size
- Some vendors may ask you for your name and address even when you pay in cash – respectfully decline
- Always inform the parties with whom you do business that you do not want your name added to mailing lists

DEALING WITH REPEAT OFFENDERS

- If a postage paid reply envelope is included, use it to request that your name be removed from the company's lists
- Review the company's literature or website to see if there is an 0800 number you can use to make such a request at no cost
- Write the words 'return to sender' on the communication you've received, and underneath add the message, 'Please remove me from your mailing list now and forever' – sign it, date it, and return to the mailing list manager
- Register your name and address with the Mailing Preference Service (MPS), a free service set up by the direct marketing industry to help people who don't want to receive junk mail; contact at *www.mpsonline.org.uk*
- For more useful advice on stopping junk mail visit the Information Commissioner's Office website at *www.ico.gov.uk*

QUICK FIX: UNADDRESSED MAIL

You can reduce the amount of 'unaddressed' mail you receive by registering with the Royal Mail's door to door opt-out service (unfortunately this will not stop mail addressed to 'the occupier'). Email at optout@royalmail.com or write to: Freepost RRBT-ZBXB-TTTS Royal Mail Door to Door Opt Outs, Kingsmead House, Oxpens Road, Oxford, OX1 1RX

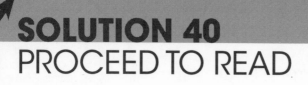

SOLUTION 40
PROCEED TO READ

It is amazing today how anyone can manage to stay organized when they are constantly being bombarded with information. Fortunately, there are techniques you can employ to assist you in completing your reading more swiftly and to help you organize and retain the information that is useful to you.

TIPS FOR MORE FOCUSED READING

Find a quiet sanctuary The fewer distractions you are surrounded by, the faster and easier you will be able to read and reflect; read early in the morning before others arrive at the office, or later in the evening when your family has retired for the night.

Skim read Simply skimming the first sentence or two is often all you need to gain the essence and to know whether you should read the material in greater depth.

Scanning through For books or a large report, review the table of contents, the foreword, any summaries, charts or graphs, reference lists and the index to determine if it merits your attention.

Evaluate the source Concentrate on only the best and most current two or three industry journals.

Read online Search for keywords that interest you to find those articles of most interest.

reading:
looking at the first
couple of sentences
of each paragraph
within an article or
chapter to assess
its suitability

RETAIN ONLY WHAT IS USEFUL TO YOU

Continually strive to keep those paper piles
as slim and trim as possible. Reduce the
paper volume to retain only the relevant
information and nothing more. Keep to hand
sticky pads, paper clips, felt-tip pens, highlighters and
scissors to assist you. When you can deftly extract
information to be retained, you can be more productive.

- If only one page of a 10 page report is
  relevant to you, ditch the rest
- Photocopy or scan just those key pages of
  a book that have value before recycling
- Use your daily commute by rail or bus
  to extract only relevant articles from
  weighty journals and reports
- If you're reading a PDF file or e-book, print
  only those pages of value to you
- Keep a titbit document of related information,
  clipping on relevant paragraphs from articles,
  website addresses or phone numbers

*in the course of a week
you may find yourself
spending anywhere
from 10 to 20 hours just
reading*

QUICK FIX: DO YOU MISS IT?
When a periodical subscription is up for renewal, let it expire with the
last issue. If you don't miss the publication, you've just saved yourself
time and money. If you do miss reading it, the publishers may even
offer you a renewal discount as a welcome back.

SUMMARY: PART FOUR RECLAIMING YOUR SPACES AND PLACES

31 **Pretend it's your first day** Imagine that you are sitting down at your desk for the first time and decide what you need and what you don't.

32 **Defeat desk clutter** When you begin each day with a clear, organized desk and a clean, organized office, you will work with more energy, focus, direction and motivation.

33 **Show your shelves who's boss** If your office shelves are crammed on the verge of collapse, you are storing items on them that should not be there.

34 **Gain power over paper** Once you have your paperwork in order you are better able to focus on more creative, fulfilling and productive work.

35 **Smile while you file** When you file items intelligently, you are able to efficiently retrieve what you need when you need it.

36   **Tickle your fancy with tickler files** You can set up a system to enable you to hold on to information for review at a later date when it is more timely to deal with it.

37   **Get clutter-busting** Take decisive action to reduce the accumulations that hold you back.

38   **Pare down and persevere** When you get rid of what you don't need, you increase the probability of succeeding in your quest to be organized.

39   **Slow the paper chase** Fight back against the constant bombardment of unsolicited junk mail at work and home.

40   **Proceed to read** Employ techniques to help you to access and retain only the information that is useful to you.

NOTES

part

five

part
five

MEETINGS, TRAVEL AND ONLINE ACTIVITIES

SOLUTION 41
CONDUCT MORE PRODUCTIVE MEETINGS

Despite the fact that many managers dislike calling meetings and staff often dread attending them, studies show that people today are spending more time in meetings than ever before.

A meeting is typically arranged by one person to convey information to many people. The hope is to share opinions, to generate ideas and to make decisions together to move projects on. But so often people shuffle into the meeting room unclear of what they are there for and unprepared to contribute.

The good news is that with just a little organization you can make your meetings more productive.

PREPARATION IS KEY

If you want to avoid thumb twiddling, text messaging, pencil tapping and daydreaming, you need to engage your participants long before the meeting starts. To do this, take just a few minutes to speak to each attendee to:

- Prepare them for what will be discussed
- Hear their views about what needs to be achieved
- Make them feel partners in the process

If your group meets on an ongoing basis, ask regular participants questions such as these:

- What methods have worked well for you in previous meetings?
- How can we proceed in a manner that involves everyone?
- What would you like to get out of this meeting?

WHAT NEXT?

There are many advantages to pre-interviewing meeting participants, not least that meeting attendees are likely to be more enthusiastic when they see that their input matters. Use the information you have learned to:

- Design a custom agenda that focuses on topics identified as important to the entire group
- Arrange the topics in an order conducive to achieving the group's overall objectives
- Circulate the agenda in advance so that participants come with ideas to contribute

---

there is no purpose in having a meeting unless the desired outcomes are known in advance

---

In his book *Breakthrough Business Meetings*, Robert Levasseur suggests that at the start of any meeting 'participants reach a common understanding of what they're going to do and how they're going to do it'. Hence, everyone needs to be ready from the get-go. Levasseur says that this normally consumes 10 per cent of the meeting time, so if you're going to be in a meeting for half an hour, use the first 3 minutes or so to deal with some basic issues, such as the main purpose of the meeting, the participants' desired outcomes and the agenda.

SOLUTION 42
KEEP MEETINGS ON TRACK

By pre-interviewing participants and issuing a meeting agenda in advance you are well on the way to conducting a meeting that is far more likely to stay on course, to have enthusiastic participant involvement, and to end the meeting on time.

Organized, competent managers know that when participants have a vested interest in the content of a meeting, they arrive promptly and are ready from the start. A well-organized agenda with time allotted to each discussion topic will help to keep a meeting on track.

CONDUCTING THE MEETING

As meeting chair it is your responsibility to start the meeting on time, follow the agenda and elicit the input of others as needed, encouraging attendees to participate. As each agenda item is discussed, ask participants to keep in mind the following questions:

- What is the specific issue being discussed?
- What does the group want to accomplish in discussing this issue?
- What action needs to be taken to handle it?
- Who will act?
- What types of resource are required?
- When will the issue be resolved?
- When will the group discuss the results?

Upon successful conclusion of these questions, the group then moves on to the next issue. (These questions are unnecessary when an agenda item is an announcement or report to the group.)

KEEPING MEETINGS TIMELY

We all know how frustrating it can be to attend a meeting that drags on way beyond its finish time. To avoid this:

- Encourage participants to circulate any supporting materials in advance for reading beforehand and to deliver only a brief summary of these at the meeting itself
- Remind attendees to keep their remarks within the allotted time frames – make sure the meeting room has a working clock that everyone can see
- As each topic comes up for discussion, announce who will be speaking next and how many minutes have been allocated
- Ask participants to stand at their chairs when they speak – this generally limits the time they will speak for
- Encourage meeting participants to arrive early and stay late so that any 'catching up' with colleagues can be done out of the meeting
- If a participant can't attend, request that they submit what they would have said in a concise paragraph to be read by someone in attendance

QUICK FIX: STARTING MEETINGS ON TIME

Here are a couple of great tips to encourage promptness:

Incentivize early arrival Hand out the best assignments in the first few minutes so that latecomers are left with the least desirable tasks.

Never backtrack for latecomers If they have to struggle to catch up they are less likely to be late next time, and you will be showing respect for those who did arrive promptly.

SOLUTION 43
CONGREGATE TO ACCOMPLISH

It is your aim to facilitate a meeting environment in which the participants have the greatest chance of achieving their objectives. And, for those items on the agenda that have a corresponding action, it is your responsibility to track the progress, otherwise it will all have been a collective waste of time.

THE MEETING ENVIRONMENT

Provide a well-lit, well-ventilated meeting room If your choices are between a room slightly too warm or slightly too cool, opt for the cool one; a cool room will keep participants alert.

Provide stationery requirements If notes need to be made, provide flat surfaces and also pens and pads.

Provide refreshments and schedule breaks If the meeting is longer than an hour, provide water, tea and coffee, and allow for a 5-minute comfort break each hour.

Minimize disturbances You don't want to be disturbed by ringing phones, people knocking on the door, or any other intrusions.

Comfortable surroundings At the very least provide supportive seating; ideally choose a room with wall-to-wall carpeting and picture-adorned walls.

Technical support Set up and check out any equipment required well in advance and make sure you have a back up to cover you if things go wrong.

RECORDING AND FEEDBACK

What is discussed and agreed at the meeting must be recorded. In some groups, the secretary or transcriber takes notes on everything that is being said; others use a digital recorder and have the notes transcribed afterwards. The important thing is that the agreed actions of the meeting are distributed as soon as possible and ideally within 24 hours.

The meeting minutes need to address the question: What else needs to be accomplished, by whom and by when, to meet the overall objective? As with any goal or objective, these need to be written down, quantified and assigned specific time frames.

listening to and acting on feedback from participants can lead to more effective meetings

QUICK FIX: VIRTUAL MEETINGS
For conference calls or webinars
- Vary your voice tone, rate and inflection to keep your audience interested and engaged
- Say something loud, or twice, for emphasis
- Don't be afraid to pause, especially if you'd like the participants to reflect upon what you have said
- Address out-of-the-room attendees directly from time to time, saying 'for those listening from afar . . .'

For real-time video, such as webcams or virtual meeting projectors
- Exaggerate your facial gestures to keep your presentation lively
- Engage with your audience – lean in toward the camera on occasion
- Have visuals and graphics ready in advance and in sequence
- Keep the meeting moving at a brisk pace

SOLUTION 44
ORGANIZE FOR THE DRIVE

It is estimated that over 70 per cent of journeys to work in Great Britain are taken by car or van, and yet when you're driving a car, even at a snail's pace, your principal activity is driving. So, is it possible to make your drive to work more productive?

There is no doubt that for stress-free driving you need to organize your vehicle; keep it full of petrol, well-serviced and well-maintained, to ensure you get to work safely on a daily basis.

It is illegal to drive in the UK while using a hand-held mobile phone. Hands-free phones may be used, but they are ultimately a distraction and a driver is still open to a charge of careless driving should a police officer think they are driving poorly whilst using one.

the National Travel Survey (Department for Transport, 2006) found that one fifth of miles travelled in Great Britain was due to commuting

A study published by the *New England Journal of Medicine* showed that driving while speaking on a mobile phone makes a driver four times as likely to get into an accident and 11 times as likely to be killed while driving. It's as dangerous as driving drunk.

MAKE THE MOST OF THE DRIVE

Source interesting books and inspiring lectures on CD You can safely listen to audio as you drive.

Car share with a colleague It will save you money and you'll have someone to bounce ideas off.

Turn to a classical music radio station The rhythms and composition have been shown to promote healing and well being.

Turn off the radio Use driving time for reflection and organize your thoughts on the way to work.

Visualize your success Consider what's on your agenda for the morning, what you'll be doing, whom you'll be meeting, and then see yourself successfully handling it all.

QUICK FIX: ERRANDS ON THE GO

Instead of letting your errands stack up for the weekend, designate one night a week as 'errand night' and make time to deal with them on the way back from work.

- Make a brief list of jobs and fix it to your dashboard
- Keep a folder or envelope handy to keep coupons, receipts, etc, in
- Buy in multiples so you don't have to return to various stores as often
- If you encounter traffic jams, go home and deal with your errands another day

SOLUTION 45
COMMUTE ASTUTELY

If you find that you are more often stuck in a traffic jam than on the go when commuting to work, talk to your boss about flexible working hours. If you start your journey an hour or so earlier than everyone else, or an hour or so later, your trip is likely to be quicker and less stressful.

Is it possible to work from home for an hour or so before departing for the office? Or maybe you can leave work early in the afternoon, and then continue with your work at home? It is certainly worth discussing.

TRAVEL WISE

If you are travelling at odd hours or on long journeys, keep these useful things in the car:

- A spare set of house keys in case everyone is out or asleep on your return
- A bag of change (hidden) to use for parking meters and vending machines
- A car charger for your mobile phone
- A backup briefcase or folder in your boot containing stamps, envelopes, pens, paper, a calculator and a list of important phone numbers
- An overnight bag just in case
- Inclement weather gear including an umbrella, raincoat, hat, gloves
- First-aid kit and a flashlight

QUICK FIX: STAY HOME
Talk to your manager and see if it is possible to work from home once a week or every other week. Get wired to your office by fax, Internet and telephone if you're not already.

SOLUTION 46
TRAVEL TO WORK WITH A PURPOSE

Many people travel to work by public transport. If you are travelling at the height of the rush hour the journey can be packed, making it difficult to read a paper or work on your laptop. If these activities prove impossible, there are still plenty of others that you can engage in to pass the time productively.

TRAVEL COMPANIONS

MP3 player Music can help to tune out surrounding noise on buses and trains. Alternatively, find motivational lectures that support how you want to be and feel in life.

if you engross yourself in an activity you can make the time pass more quickly

Laptop or notebook computer These are only really workable if you can get a seat, ideally on the non-sunny side; make sure they are fully charged up just in case. To avoid becoming a ready-made target for thieves, transport in a satchel or battered briefcase, rather than a sleek computer carrying case.

Ebook reader Ideal for reading books and newspaper articles when space is limited.

Mobile phone Great for staying in touch while on the move but do be respectful of other passengers; turn away from the open area, modulate your voice, and keep your conversations as short as possible.

Handheld scanners Ideal for scanning important titbits of information gleaned from magazine articles, newspapers and books read on your travels.

SOLUTION 47
THE FEARLESS FLYER

With ever increasing air traffic, more restrictive airline configuration, and heightened and tightened security, you need to get yourself organized and take care of as many things as you can in advance when travelling by plane for business.

TRAVEL LIGHT

If travelling on a business trip, it makes sense to travel as light as you can. Try to restrict yourself to carry-on luggage only if possible as this can save you a good 15 to 20 minutes prior to your departure and upon arrival at your destination.

if you do have to pack a second bag, use something that fits on the top of your rolling cart luggage

- Check the size of the carry-on luggage for the airline you are using
- It is usually 56cm x 46cm x 25cm (22in x 18in x 10in) with a weight limit of approximately 10kg, but there will be variations between airlines
- When practical, mail things ahead rather than pack them
- Make sure your toiletries are in less than100ml sizes and that you have the requisite self-seal plastic bag to keep them in
- Use rolling luggage to avoid having to lift your belongings

AIRPORT DOS AND DON'TS

for more useful advice on travel visit the British & Foreign Commonwealth Office on www.fco.gov.uk

Do use the self-service check-in whenever possible.

Do aim for frequent passenger status to speed through the baggage check.

Do be prepared for your encounter with the security checkpoint – have your passport and toiletries ready, and take off your shoes and jewellery.

Don't become your security line's bottleneck by being unprepared to stroll through the metal detector.

Don't dispute with the security official about what can and cannot be taken on to the plane – find out beforehand.

QUICK FIX: TWO GREAT PACKING TIPS

Tip 1 For longer trips with many stops pack enough clothes for half the trip plus one day, so for a nine-day trip, pack five days' clothing. As you approach the halfway point, make use of hotel laundering services. It may cost a little but is better than toting around a bulky bag of heavy and increasingly dirty clothing.

Tip 2 Don't pack anything that the hotel supplies. Call in advance to get the list of what is offered. It can save a lot of space in your case if you don't have to pack a bathrobe, an alarm clock, a hairdryer and other overnight necessities.

SOLUTION 48
ARRIVE IN BETTER SHAPE

By making adequate preparations in advance when travelling by air, you can ensure that you have the most comfortable journey possible, arriving at your destination in the best possible shape to do business.

AIR TRAVELLER'S CHECK LIST

make the best use of your time on board and try to get the best possible seat you can

√ Ask for a bulkhead, wing row, or aisle seat – all have more room than a middle or window seat.

√ Carry an empty water bottle with you to fill up after the security check point to avoid having to wait for the crew's first refreshment round – it is important to keep well hydrated to be productive.

√ Bring your own healthy, energy-boosting snacks, such as carrots, cucumbers, apples, bananas, sunflower seeds and peanuts, in preference to the high-carbohydrate offerings provided by your airline.

√ Wear loose, comfortable clothing – sitting in an airplane seat is confining so avoid heavy jumpers, tight shoes, restrictive belts, and anything else that hampers your breathing and circulation.

√ If you are flying at midday when the sun's ultraviolet rays are more pronounced, carry sunglasses with you – also use the airline overhead lighting and lower your window cover to prevent your eyes from getting fatigued.

SOLUTION 49
MANAGE WEB RESEARCH EFFECTIVELY

The Internet has all but taken over as our dominant entertainment, communication and information resource, and ever more user-friendly applications are becoming available all the time.

The Internet is a great tool for keeping up with what is going on in your particular field of business, but if you are not careful it can be a major drain on your time and energy.

MAKE THE INTERNET WORK FOR YOU

Although any specific program cited will be quickly replaced, there are two broad categories of service-orientated sites that can facilitate your Internet research saving you time and money.

Bots Download one from websites such as *www.botspot.com* and it will search the Internet all day long, giving you the best possible prices and best deals for the products and services you're seeking. Some of the most popular bots available ferret out information on shopping, health and travel.

make sure you institute an effective backup routine to prevent losing important electronic information

Electronic clipping services 'Clipping' services, including www.burrellesluce.com and www.cyberclipping.com, offer you highly customized topic searches for a fee. Such sites can generate nearly everything that appears on the entire web on any single day about a given company or topic.

SOLUTION 50
KEEP EMAIL UNDER CONTROL

You send and receive emails all day long. Email is fast – it's transmitted nearly instantaneously after you push the send button. Unlike making a phone call or writing a letter, it is a one-action task, which is why you receive so many every day – it's too convenient.

You can send anything to anybody, and the reverse is true of course, which explains why, when you spend just a brief time away from your computer, your inbox fills up with emails.

EFFECTIVE EMAIL MANAGEMENT

If you receive a large volume of email traffic you must learn to triage it. This involves allocating emails into three categories based on what needs to be handled immediately, what can be handled later, and what can be ignored altogether.

Category 1 Eliminate the obvious junk including all forms of spam.

Category 2 Pick out non-urgent emails you can place in a holding folder till later – this may include messages from friends and loved ones, which would be better read over at leisure.

Category 3 Those emails that require your immediate action. These may not necessarily be urgent, but they may prompt you into action; after all if you're able to respond to a request quickly and effortlessly, why waste time parking it?

KEEPING ON TOP OF YOUR EMAIL

Many of your stored email messages become redundant the moment you receive a current message, so it's easier to stay organized by dealing with your emails as you receive them rather than having to face a daunting number of unsorted messages.

- Triage your email (see opposite) to identify Category 3 'Deal with now' emails; tackle the most important first, such as those from your customers and your boss
- Use your email software's filtering systems more effectively – set it up to sort, respond to, and delete messages; maintain a list of your top priority contacts, direct everything else out of your inbox, and weed out unwelcome known addresses
- If possible, delegate a response – others may be better informed to deal with the query
- If any email demands your attention, handle it at once to prevent it from continuing to distract you
- Mark an urgency level on the messages you send and encourage your colleagues and staff to use this feature appropriately too

QUICK FIX: BEAT THE SPAMMERS

Make yourself invisible to spammers. Change your email format. For example, the email address Jeff@BreathingSpace.com can alternatively be written as Jeff(at)BreathingSpace.com. This format appears enough like a standard email address for most people to understand, but spammers will pass right over it.

SUMMARY: PART FIVE
MEETINGS, TRAVEL AND
ONLNE ACITIVITIES

41   **Conduct more productive meetings** If you want to avoid thumb twiddling, text messaging, pencil tapping and daydreaming, you need to engage your participants long before the meeting starts.

42   **Keep meetings on track** A well-organized agenda with time allotted to each discussion topic will help to keep a meeting on track.

43   **Congregate to accomplish** You need to facilitate a meeting environment in which the participants have the greatest chance of achieving their objectives, and you must ensure the identified actions are followed up on.

44   **Organize for the drive** It is possible to make your drive to work more productive.

45   **Commute astutely** If flexible working hours are possible for your role, your journey time could be quicker and less stressful, leaving you more productive.

46   **Travel to work with a purpose** It is possible to pass the time productively when commuting on packed public transport.

47   **The fearless flyer** Get yourself organized and take care of as many things as you can in advance when travelling by plane for business.

48   **Arrive in better shape** Make preparations to guarantee a comfortable journey so that you arrive at your destination ready for business.

49   **Manage web research effectively** The Internet is a great tool for keeping up with what is going on in your particular field of business, but guard against it draining your time and energy.

50   **Keep email under control** If you receive a large volume of email traffic you need to manage it effectively.

NOTES

part
six

part
six

MAKING YOUR HOME YOUR CASTLE

SOLUTION 51
RECLAIM YOUR SPACES

'Have nothing in your house that you do not know to be useful, or believe to be beautiful.'
William Morris

Today our homes are simply inundated with too many things competing for our time and attention. When too many items are crammed into a physical space you can start to feel out of control. Things get mislaid and your energy gets zapped.

By reclaiming the spaces in your home, you can find things faster and easier, be more efficient and have greater peace of mind.

the more organized you are at home, the more focus and energy you will have at work

SET UP A PROCESSING STATION

Getting organized starts when you come in the door. Anything you bring into your home should be processed before being moved on to its end destination. This is a sure-fire way to prevent those burdensome piles from taking hold. Whether it is your hallway floor or your kitchen table, your processing station is merely a space to assess where things belong before taking them there straightaway.

Keep surfaces clear, such as the dining room table, the kitchen counter, your desk and any small tables, so that you can better manage the flow of items in and out of your life.

when returning from a trip, unpack your bags, put clothes in the wardrobe or washer, and take paperwork to your administration outpost

SET UP AN ADMINISTRATION OUTPOST

Any paperwork that enters your home also needs to be processed, and the best idea is to set up an administration outpost to help you do this. If you have a home office, this may be the ideal location to process papers; alternatively dedicate any small flat surface area to congregate papers ready for processing each and every day.

QUICK FIX: PILE BUSTING

Keep a small cabinet or table by the door, but use it only for what is leaving your home, never for what is entering. What enters goes directly to its final destination or your administration outpost. And what is exiting should depart soon. The process of moving stuff out should be continual, just like at work.

if mornings are a mad rush pack your car with everything you and your family need the night before so nothing gets forgotten

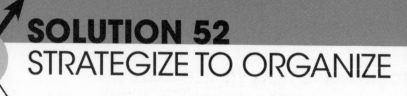

SOLUTION 52
STRATEGIZE TO ORGANIZE

You need to train yourself to think strategically when approaching your spaces at home. Consider the space you have and how it can best be used for the purpose it has been assigned.

if you approach your storage strategically, you can devise orderly systems to serve you well

THE EXAMPLE OF THE LINEN CUPBOARD

When you open your linen cupboard you should be able to open the door and have exactly what you need, be it a bath sheet or a bed sheet, at your fingertips. In reality, what is more likely to happen is that blankets and oversized towels tumble down on top of you. Strategic planning can result in perfect order – for example:

- Keep the same items together on the same shelf – single bed sheets on one shelf, double bed sheets on another, pillowcases on another
- Store towels of the same size together to ensure stable piles
- Stow frequently-used items on the most accessible shelves
- Use the far recesses of the cupboard to store excess-to-requirement supplies
- Store related items such as cleaning materials or toiletries, or electrical items such as a hairdryer and foot massager, here too
- Use the height of shelves to determine what goes where – children's washcloths on lower shelves, for example, but extra cleaning supplies on the highest shelves out of the reach of small hands

CONTINUE TO THINK STRATEGICALLY

Apply strategic thinking to other areas of your home. Here are a few solutions to the all-too-common problem of not being able to see the floor of your wardrobe for the covering of shoes.

- Buy a stacking ready-built shoe shelf for the base of your wardrobe
- Utilize old wine racks to hold pairs of shoes
- Buy mesh shoe bags so you can see what is contained inside, and hang from hooks on the back of the wardrobe door
- Buy a dedicated 'shoe organizing' system from a home store to fit your wardrobe's dimensions
- Have a shoe review and give away those that you don't wear anymore

QUICK FIX: SEASONAL STORAGE

If your wardrobe space is limited, rotate its contents according to the needs of the season. As spring approaches, box up all the winter items and put them in the attic, the basement, or in airtight storage bags beneath the bed. Always store clothes laundered and pressed ready for the next season. Repeat this exercise every three months.

SOLUTION 53
DIVIDE AND CONQUER

Many people have a place in their home – a box room, a spare cupboard, the utility room or the attic – that they use as a dumping ground for all the things they don't have a dedicated space for. But all too often this becomes just a cluttered mess – unless decisive action is taken, there is little chance of locating anything here either quickly or easily.

The key to bringing order to such a space in your home is to divide up the items and create permanent separations – the divide and conquer principle.

the divide and conquer principle is essential for dealing with mess beyond reason and hope

FIRST DIVIDE

Dumping ground spaces can contain a diverse range of items including tennis balls, wires, excess telephone cords, gloves, mittens, nuts and bolts, flashlights, batteries, as well as some objects whose purpose has long been forgotten. Your first job is to separate these into groups of similar items.

Equip yourself with as many empty shoeboxes or small containers as you can find, and begin to put like items together. For example, place all the balls into one container – tennis balls, racket balls, ping-pong balls and golf balls; in another, put all the small electrical stuff including wires, phone cords, extensions, extra light switches, wall outlets. For the handful of items that seem to go with no others, put in a 'miscellaneous' box.

THEN CONQUER

Now that you have sorted the items into groups of similar things, revisit these and ask yourself:

Does this belong somewhere else? Relocate any items that do belong elsewhere.

Is this still usable? Throw away anything that is obsolete or irreparably damaged.

Do I need this? Give away duplicate items to family, friends or charity stores.

VANQUISH CLUTTER

Now that you have sorted the items into groups and decided what you need to keep, you are ready to organize what remains into the space you have. You need to be strategic about this (see Solution 52). The chances are that you only have a limited amount of space so make the most of it.

- Buy shelves to fit the space you have – those with adjustable shelves are best
- In the space between the floor and the bottom of the first shelf, place the largest items so that there is less danger of injury from falling objects
- On higher shelves, place the lightest items, those seldom used, and objects that can be easily seen by the smallest members of the family
- Let the borders between containers serve as compartments – this is ideal for piles of fabric or clothes, or cans and canisters that must remain upright

SOLUTION 54
STORE CREATIVELY WHEN SPACE IS SPARSE

Face it, you will never have all the space you need. The worse possible thing you can do is to fall into the trap of overloading the storage spaces in and around your home. And yet so many people do this. It starts off harmless enough, and for the first few months or even years, everything seems orderly. But before you know it, these spaces are jam-packed with clutter and you are back to square one.

take control of your storage spaces now before anyone gets hurt

AN ACCIDENT WAITING TO HAPPEN

If you haven't cleaned out your storage spaces, such as the garage, the attic, or the cellar, in a long time, make time now. The sorts of items you are likely to store in places such as these – flammable materials, sharp-pointed tools – can make them hazardous to those who dare to venture in, and this is even more true when these spaces are allowed to become disorganized.

TIPS FOR MAKING STORAGE AREAS SAFER

- For cellars, attics and garages, install a light nearby on a switch or keep a dependable flashlight at the point of entry
- Don't store anything on cellar steps, as this will almost inevitably cause someone to trip and fall
- Invest in freestanding storage units if more storage space is required, and select units that are best served to do the job you require
- If floor space is limited, use the walls, but make sure that supplies, tools and other suitable items are securely fastened
- Make sure you have plenty of room to manoeuvre – you don't want to be bumping into things or tripping over them
- Maintain these easy-to-forget areas, regularly sweeping to keep clean and check for any pest infestations

make the most of the storage space you have

SOLUTION 55
SEEK OUT AN ORGANIZING SPECIALIST

If you are finding it difficult to get organized you could consider engaging the services of a professional organizer. This may be just what you need to put you on the right path, but it can be expensive. If you choose to go down this route, find an organizer who is prepared to teach you the principles of organization.

A professional organizer should work with you to examine those areas of your life that have become disorganized and to rearrange them so that they work for you, and as such you can learn a great deal from him or her.

to maintain places and spaces you must understand the principles of organization

KNOWLEDGE IS POWER

When you know the reason for putting pens to the right, paper in the top centre drawer, and so on, you have a better chance of maintaining your system. Your aim should be to maintain the systems that the professional organizer has set up for you after he or she has departed. If it makes sense to have a professional organizer help you initiate those principles visit *www.apdo-uk.co.uk* for possible contacts in your local area.

COMMIT TO A CLEANING DAY RITUAL

Once your home is in order, it should only take a couple of hours once a week to maintain it. Pick a regular day and time – popular choices are Friday evening at the end of the working week, or Saturday morning for the start of the weekend.

select a day and a time that works for you and develop an organizing maintenance routine

A typical list of chores might read:

- Put on the wash
- Vacuum the house as the washing machine goes through its cycles
- Put the clothes in the dryer
- Restore the kitchen – polish silverware, clean the sink, sweep the floor
- Take the clothes out of the dryer and fold them
- Distribute clothes to the linen cupboard and bedroom drawers, quickly straightening rooms as you do so
- Clean the bathroom

No doubt the house will be a mess again by the end of the week but this need not stress you out as you have committed to a regular day and time to put things in order again.

Many business people devote some part of Friday afternoon to 'office housekeeping', a regular day and time to restore order. Why Friday? Many people find it hard to stay focused as the last few hours of the working week wind down, so this is a good way to keep usefully busy. They can then leave for the weekend having a sense of control.

SOLUTION 56
EMPLOY THE REPLACEMENT PRINCIPLE

As you begin to regain some order at home, there is a practical way to stop your possessions from accumulating and engulfing you once again. You must employ the replacement principle: that is, when you acquire something new, something else must be got rid of.

you've got enough to deal with in the present without the clutter of the past

If you're not constantly reducing what you're holding on to, you are in danger of undoing all the good work you have done in organizing your home. Don't let stuff take control again; stay in control of it. Be vigilant and guard against complacency. You've got enough to deal with in the present; who needs the clutter of the past along with it?

The chart on the opposite page will help you to identify 'good' replacement policies from 'bad' non-replacement ones.

the replacement principle: when you acquire something new, something else has to go

NON-REPLACEMENT	REPLACEMENT
Your child's collection of DVDs grows beyond 50 as you acquire the classics as well as all the latest hits.	You decide with your child in advance on a total number of DVDs; each new one means replacing an old one.
Your files keep growing until you need to buy another filing cabinet.	Your files stay the same size because for each item you add, you discard one.
Old equipment is stored in spare cupboards (until you have no cupboards spare) in case of future value.	When you buy new equipment, youdonate older equipment to a charitable organization.
You've collected books since college and you now have overflowing shelves with no hope of reading most of what you've collected.	You retain only books of continuing or sentimental value. You quickly scan or copy pages important to you from surplus books, before passing on to friends to enjoy.
Although you have a 284GB hard disk, you are considering getting more disk space.	You don't need any additional hard disk space because you routinely prune your disk of outdated files.
Your chest of drawers and wardrobes are overfilled, mostly with items you haven't worn in years.	There is more than sufficient space to house the clothes that you actually use, because you give the rest to charities.
You have memorabilia from your last trip, and many previous trips as well.	You have a few choice mementos from your last few trips; you choose to display some of them and store the rest.
Your record collection spans many shelves and is covered with dust; you hardly ever play them.	You sell or donate LPs and you buy a few 'greatest hits' CDs; you download only those songs you will play.

SOLUTION 57
BUY GIFTS WITH A GAME PLAN

It can be difficult to buy presents for some people, but the closer you leave it to the day, the more stressful it can become, and the more likely you will be to buy an unsuitable gift.

at Christmas keep wrapped 'his' and 'her' gifts to reciprocate in case of unexpected presents from visiting guests

Adjusting how and when you shop can make buying gifts less stressful for you. With a little bit of organization you can increase your chances of buying a present that will be appreciated but that won't break your bank account.

SAVVY SHOPPING TIPS

- Create a year-round gift list to ease the burden of shopping at Christmas and birthdays – when a friend comments on something he likes or she, make note of it
- Choose the days you shop carefully – Mondays and Tuesdays are much less crowded than the weekends
- For faraway friends, choose easy-to-post gifts such as DVDs, CDs, gift certificates, and jewellery – it also makes shopping a lot lighter experience
- At Christmas take advantage of free present-wrapping offered by some stores – one less thing to do when you get home
- Reuse gift bags after removing any personal messages first – wrap your gift in tissue paper and tie a new gift tag onto the handle for a fast wrapping

THE GIFT CERTIFICATE

keep all price tags and receipts in one place where they are easy to find in case you need to take a gift back

Contrary to popular belief the gift certificate is not just the resort of the last-minute shopper. Sometimes, it can represent the most thoughtful of gifts for family and friends.

iTunes gift card They can download their favourite songs and when they listen to them on their MP3 player, they'll think of you.

Hobby store gift card They can put it towards taking a class or buying supplies, and they will be touched that you noticed their passion.

Book tokens You can include a few Amazon reviews of books you think that they might like.

QUICK FIX: SHOPPING AT CHRISTMAS
- When out and about for Christmas shopping, pick up a few extra items for friends and family who have birthdays only a few months away
- Buy next year's Christmas essentials – wrapping paper, greeting cards, bows, crackers – at great reductions in the New Year's sales

SOLUTION 58
GET ORGANIZED TO BUY

Prior to stepping foot in a store or ordering something online, you need to determine exactly what you want from the product you are purchasing. If you wait until you are on the showroom floor to ascertain the functions and features you require, you may not be assured of getting the best deal for you.

Just as important as the benefits and the features of the purchased item are those provided by the company you are buying it from. Once again, a little research really pays off.

THE PURCHASER'S CHECK LIST

Outlined opposite are check lists of the sorts of services you might require from the companies you buy from. The questions have been developed to help you to get the best deal and offer you a springboard for discussion before you buy.

QUICK FIX: HOME SHOPPING

There is so much you can do without leaving home nowadays, at any time of the day and night, all from your desktop computer. You can:

- Buy stamps
- Transfer cash from one bank account to another
- Renew and reserve library books
- Research goods, services and products
- Order groceries for home delivery

Discounts

- Are there quantity discounts or special terms?
- Are there corporate, government, association or educational discounts?
- Do they give weekly, monthly or seasonal discounts?
- Do they offer frequent buyer discounts?
- Do they give off-peak discounts or odd-lot discounts?
- Do they offer a guaranteed lowest price?

Ordering options

- Do they accept major credit cards or debit cards?
- Do they accept orders by fax or by email?
- Do they offer a money-back guarantee or other guarantees?
- Do they have a free-to-call ordering line and a customer service line?
- Is it easy to reach a live operator?
- Can you order online instead of going into the store?

Delivery

- Do they guarantee the dispatch date?
- Do they offer free delivery and installation?
- How long for delivery?
- What else is included?

Other considerations

- How long have they been in business?
- Are there authorized dealer/repair services in your area?
- Does the product come with a warranty?

SOLUTION 59
BE A SMART SHOPPER

Once you have done your research online you are ready to visit the stores to try your product shortlist out on site. With a piece of paper in hand with your top choices listed, you have organized yourself to give yourself the best chance of buying the product which has the capabilities that you need.

visit a store to give your selected appliances a good workout

GATHER INFORMATION

Always visit the store with the mindset that you are there to gather information, not necessarily to buy. Remember the salesperson is present to serve you, so make sure he does just that.

To save your time wading through thick instruction manuals, get the salesperson to talk you through how to operate each unit and to run through its functions while you are in the store so that you can compare them.

QUICK FIX: KEEP IT SIMPLE

Fewer switches, buttons or dials may not mean that a product is less sophisticated or offers fewer benefits or features. In fact, the opposite may be true. Rather than the full instruction manual, ask to see the at-a-glance instructions. Condensed on to a single page or card, often laminated, these list the basic functions most regularly used.

SHORTCUT TO SUCCESS

Taking the simple instruction card in hand, see how easily you can operate the showroom model. Run through the card once with the salesperson's help, then a second time without it. If you can master what is on the card, then you have found a possible contender.

seek products and instructions designed for the consumer

With the salesperson standing by, run through the sequence of steps as if you had already purchased the machine. Understanding exactly how the appliance works will save you so much effort when you are at home on your own, with no guidance and only a 180-page instruction manual to help you. When you take the time to have the instructions explained to you – repeatedly if necessary – you can't possibly fail.

If you can't get the hang of an appliance on the second run-through, it may be time to move on to another make or model, one that is easier to operate but still performs the basic functions that you are seeking.

FINISH THE PAPERWORK

When you have made your final purchase and it is installed at home, do make sure you:

- Fill in and post the warranty card
- File the receipt, diagrams or schematics, and any other associated paperwork
- Keep the instruction manual and the at-a-glance instructions near the appliance

SOLUTION 60
STAY ON TOP OF YOUR TAXES

Keeping accurate, complete tax information is a must in the life of the organized individual who has to fill in a tax return each year. If this applies to you, you can take simple steps to ensure that you have the documents necessary to back you up, relaxing in the knowledge that your financial affairs are in good order.

RECORD KEEPING

When needing to keep documents, receipts and vouchers relating to both your income and your expenses, as with most organizational tasks, simplicity is best. Some

it is important to keep a track of your income and your business expenses throughout the year

people maintain their records in a concertina folder with a compartment for each month of the year. Others invest in more involved folders allowing them to file receipts, etc, on a weekly basis over the course of 52 weeks. For most though, the three-ring binder system works well.

Insert dividers for each month, add three-hole punched plastic sleeves so you can both store and view the receipts and documentation you accumulate. If your expenditures in any given month are considerable, simply use more than one sheet for that month. There is usually more than enough room in your binder to hold any specific information relating to your circumstances.

KEEPING ACCOUNT

There are a few common practices that can make filling in your tax return a good deal easier:

- Open a separate business account for business income paid in and business expenses paid out
- Open a savings account and connect it up to your business account; transfer sufficient funds to cover your basic tax and NI contributions every time an invoice is paid
- Make all major business purchases using a credit card used only for this purpose
- Always ask for a receipt when making any business purchase
- Write directly on to the receipt the details of the purchase
- When it is not possible to get a receipt for out-of-pocket expenses, keep details in a cash book (pick one up from your local post office)
- Leave plenty of time to fill in your tax return before the due date and set aside a day to do so

QUICK FIX: FILING ONLINE

It may be possible to file your tax return online, and this gives you an extra three months to do so. For more information visit *www.hmrc.gov.uk*

SUMMARY: PART SIX
MAKING YOUR HOME
YOUR CASTLE

51   **Reclaim your spaces** If you manage the flow of items in and out of your home, you will be more efficient and have greater peace of mind.

52   **Strategize to organize** Consider the space you have and how it can best be used for the purpose it has been assigned.

53   **Divide and conquer** Bring order to 'dumping ground' spaces in your home by dividing up the items and creating permanent separations.

54   **Store creatively when space is sparse** Don't fall into the trap of overloading the storage spaces in and around your home.

55   **Seek an organizing specialist** To maintain your places and spaces you must understand the principles of organization and a professional organizer may have much to teach you.

56 **Employ the replacement principle** When you acquire something new, something else must be got rid of.

57 **Buy gifts with a game plan** With a little bit of organization you can increase your chances of buying a gift that will be appreciated but that won't break your bank account.

58 **Get organized to buy** Take time to research the functions and features of the goods and services you want to buy and the best companies to buy them from.

59 **Be a smart shopper** Visit a store to give your selected appliances a good workout and to get the salespeople to show you how to get the most from your purchases.

60 **Stay on top of your taxes** Take simple steps to ensure that your financial affairs are in good order.

NOTES

FURTHER READING

Archibald, D Russell, *Managing High-Technology Programs and Projects* (Wiley, 1998)

Aslett, Don, *Clutter Free Finally and Forever* (Marsh Creek Press, 1995)

Cathcart, Jim, *The Acorn Principle* (St Martin's Press, 1998)

Culbertson, Judi, *The Clutter Cure* (McGraw-Hill, 2007)

Davidson, Jeff, *Breathing Space* (Booksurge, 2007)

Davidson, Jeff, *The Complete Idiot's Guide to Getting Things Done* (Alpha Books, 2005)

Davidson, Jeff, *The Complete Idiot's Guide to Managing Your Time* (Alpha Books, 2002)

Davidson, Jeff, *60 Second Solutions Motivation* (David & Charles, 2011)

Eisenberg, Ronni, *Organize Your Life: Free Yourself From Clutter and Find More Personal Time* (Wiley, 2007)

Felton, Sandra, *Messies Manual* (Fleming Revel, 1983)

Fritz, Robert, *The Path of Least Resistance* (Ballantine, 1989)

Hall, Edward, *The Hidden Dimension* (Doubleday, 1966)

Hemphill, Barbara, *Taming the Paper Tiger* (Kiplinger Books, 1996)

Kostner, Jaclyn, *Knights for the TeleRound Table* (Warner, 1994)

Levasseur, Robert, *Breakthrough Business Meetings* (Adams Media, 1994)

Markham, Ursula, *The Elements of Visualization* (Element Books, 1989)

Maslow, Abraham, *Toward a Psychology of Being* (Wiley, 1968)

Moore-Ede, Martin, *The Twenty-Four-Hour Society* (Addison-Wesley, 1993)

Moskowitz, Robert, *How to Organize Your Work and Your Life* (Mainstream Books, 1981)

Pagonis, William, *Moving Mountains* (Harvard Business School Press, 1992)

Salsbury, Glenna, *The Art of the Fresh Start* (Health Communications, 1995)

Stack, Laura, *Find More Time: How to Get Things Done at Home, Organize Your Life, and Feel Great About It* (Broadway Books, 2006)

Sugarman, Joseph, *Success Forces* (Contemporary Books, 1980)

Zeer, Darrin, *Office Yoga: Simple Stretches for Busy People* (Chronicle Books, 2000)

ABOUT THE AUTHOR

JEFF DAVIDSON is an author and professional speaker who offers new perspectives and fresh solutions to the career and life balance problems that people face today. He has been featured in the USA's top newspapers including *USA Today*, the *Washington Post*, the *New York Times*, the *Los Angeles Times*, and the *Chicago Tribune*. A five-time state winner of the US Small Business Administration's Media Advocate of the Year Award, he has published more than 3,550 articles on the topics of life-balance, management and marketing effectiveness, and time management. Corporate clients who have benefited from his expertise include America Online, Lufthansa, Wells Fargo, NationsBank, IBM, Swissotel, Executone, American Express, and more than 500 other leading organizations and associations including the US Treasury.

Jeff is a columnist in three publications, an audio columnist on Selling Power Live, and a frequent Webinar presenter for the Manage Smarter, Audio Educators, and Apex Performance Systems. In the highly competitive field of self-help, business, and how-to books, sales of his books exceed over 100,000 copies sold in the last five years alone, and his output includes such popular titles as: *The Joy of Simple Living*, *The Complete Guide to Public Speaking*, *Breathing Space* and *The Complete Idiot's Guide to Time Management*.

For more information on Jeff and his work visit *www.Breathing-Space.com* or contact him by email at Jeff@BreathingSpace.com.

INDEX